The Three Pillars

"Upon three things the world is based: upon the Torah, upon divine service, and upon deeds of loving-kindness."

(Ethics of the Fathers 1:2)

The Three Pillars

Thought, Worship and Practice
for the Jewish Woman

By

DEBORAH M. MELAMED

Thought · Worship · Practice

THE NATIONAL WOMEN'S LEAGUE
OF THE UNITED SYNAGOGUE OF AMERICA
3080 BROADWAY, NEW YORK 27, NEW YORK

1958–5718

© 1927 by

THE NATIONAL WOMEN'S LEAGUE

Reprinted

1931, 1936, 1940, 1942, 1946, 1949, 1954

© Revised Edition, 1958

PRINTED IN THE UNITED STATES OF AMERICA
PRESS OF *Maurice Jacobs* INC.
224 N. 15TH ST., PHILADELPHIA 2, PENNA.

AUTHOR'S PREFACE

The Three Pillars does not attempt an exhaustive study of Jewish philosophy or practice. It confines itself to presenting some all-pervading Jewish ideals and some understandings which should be familiar to every Jewish woman. It seeks to show also, how the spirit of Judaism and its historic ideals have found expression through the ages, in outward symbols and ceremonies.

To those who do not know this inner spirit or cannot understand its expressions, these ceremonies and symbols may seem out of touch with the modern scene, and as lifeless as the dry bones viewed in the valley by the prophet Ezekiel. But to those who are able to interpret their message, they are eloquent with significance and appeal. They can still fire the imagination and enthrall the heart.

It is to promote such deeper perception of the meaning of Jewish practices and observances that this book has been written. When the modern Jewish woman attains this new insight she will again invest these time-honored outward expressions of the Jewish soul with their proper importance in molding and preserving Jewish existence. She will then take pride in creating for herself and for her family, as the generations before her have done, an observant and richly rewarding Jewish life.

To the ladies who formed the Book Committee, Mrs. Moses Hyamson, the Chairman, Mrs. Louis Ginzberg, Mrs. Charles I. Hoffman, Mrs. Jacob Hoschander, Mrs. Jacob Kohn, Mrs. Alexander Marx, Mrs. Leon Solis-Cohen and to Miss Rose A. Herzog, my thanks are due for ever so many helpful suggestions and for careful reading of the proofs.

Deborah M. Melamed

FOREWORD

A great deal has happened to the world, and to the Jewish people, in the more than thirty years since the late Deborah Melamed prepared this comprehensive guide for the Jewish homemaker. That the book has continued to be useful is attested to by the fact that this will be its ninth printing; that the passage of a whole generation should have created a need for some revision was only to be expected. In response to this need, the National Women's League with the assistance of its Reading and Editorial Committee has prepared this new edition of THE THREE PILLARS.

Actually, the revisions have been kept to a minimum. Apart from the ordinary orthographical considerations — such as changing fashions in the transliteration of Hebrew words — the editors have given their attention to a few shifts in emphasis with regard to Jewish home rituals; and have at the same time added references to some of the newer observances current in American synagogues, like the *Bat Mitzvah* ceremony for girls, Consecration services, and so on.

None of this, of course, can reflect the two great changes that have come over Jewish life in recent

FOREWORD

decades. Of one of these — the destruction of one third of the Jewish people — much needs to be said, but not here. The other great change — the emergence of the State of Israel — can scarcely be left unrelated to a book of thought, worship and practice for Jewish women.

It should, therefore, be stated explicitly, that Judaism as here described is inconceivable without a concept of the Jewish people; and equally inconceivable without a special place in its world of thought and action for the Land of Israel. All of this is implicit in every home observance, in the Hebrew of every *Berachah*, in the descriptions of Bible and Prayer Book. The rebirth of Jewish creativity in the old-new Land has made these implications clearer.

More and more the Jewish woman plays an active role not only as homemaker, but also as builder of the Hebrew schools, the synagogue, and the Jewish community in its every aspect. Not least among the spheres of her interest is her affiliation with Zionist and related organizations dedicated to the strengthening of Israel.

SHONIE B. LEVI

CONTENTS

	PAGE
AUTHOR'S PREFACE	5
FOREWORD	7
CHAPTER ONE THE YEAR ROUND	15
CHAPTER TWO MILESTONES	30
CHAPTER THREE DIETARY LAWS	40
CHAPTER FOUR PRAYER	48
CHAPTER FIVE THE BIBLE	59
CHAPTER SIX SABBATH	67

CONTENTS

	PAGE
CHAPTER SEVEN ROSH HA-SHANAH	77
CHAPTER EIGHT YOM KIPPUR	90
CHAPTER NINE PESAḤ	98
CHAPTER TEN SHAVUOT	111
CHAPTER ELEVEN SUKKOT	115
CHAPTER TWELVE ḤANUKKAH	124
CHAPTER THIRTEEN PURIM	132
CHAPTER FOURTEEN TISHA B'AV	137

CONTENTS

	PAGE
CHAPTER FIFTEEN SEMI-HOLIDAYS AND MINOR FASTS	140
CHAPTER SIXTEEN DEATH	146
CHAPTER SEVENTEEN ISRAEL REBORN	153
CALENDAR — *LUAḤ*	156
INDEX	158

The Three Pillars

Chapter I

THE YEAR ROUND

AMERICAN SYMBOLS AND CEREMONIALS

Judaism does more than present a theory of life; it suggests specific ways by which that theory may be put into practice. It covers every normal aspect of life and provides for its emergencies. It concerns itself with the home and the market-place; with social contacts and social service; with the daily diet and the daily act of mercy; with experiences of joy and of sorrow. It concerns itself with all these, and with as much more as life itself is more than all these.

Judaism tries to keep certain ennobling ideas before us, always. It presents these ideas to us and keeps us mindful of them by ceremonies, signs or symbols. The use of ceremonies or signs in other aspects of life is familiar enough. We stand at attention when we hear the national hymn, to signify our agreement with the sentiments expressed therein; women and sometimes men wear wedding rings as a sign that their love and devotion are already pledged to some particular person. As Americans, we keep Independence Day and pay fitting tributes to those who formulated and established the principle of our national independence.

All these symbols serve to convey to the mind certain fixed ideas. In addition, they themselves have become time-honored because they have been closely connected with these ideas, and are the accepted media for expressing and transmitting their special message. If the red, white and blue, arranged in a certain way has no specific meaning for us, it is not due to any deficiency in the American flag. It is we who are blameworthy, in that we are ignorant of its significance. It is true other symbols might have been selected to convey the same ideas of "liberty and justice." The American flag might have been red, white and yellow. It might have been the general custom for the man only, and not the woman to wear the wedding ring, as it indeed is, in some lands. But these are not the symbols that have been in use among us. As Americans we perform the ceremonies and use the symbols of our own country. We find pleasure and take pride in conforming to its customs. It is not a mark of intellectual or ethical superiority for an American to ignore the customs and ceremonies of the American people. It bespeaks rather his ignorance of the significance of his country's time-honored traditions.

THE YEAR ROUND

JEWISH SYMBOLS AND CEREMONIES

The same thing holds true with Jewish ceremonies and customs. They, too, have become the fixed means, accepted by the Jewish people, for conveying certain ideas and emotions. These ceremonies are the expression of our Jewish life, celebrating its various events and securing the perpetuation of the ideas it holds sacred, by common observance. Many of them are born in national experience and effectively intensify historic feeling. They help the imagination by giving concrete form to what would otherwise be only an abstract idea. Ceremonies and symbols become a sort of picture language, a "picture philosophy" which at once expresses and strengthens the ideas in the mind.

Judaism seeks to remind us that God is the Creator and Ruler of the universe; that from Him all our blessings come; that He requires us, as a people, to be conscious of a special destiny and purpose. "Ye shall be holy even as I, the Lord, your God, am holy." — "A kingdom of priests and a holy nation." Judaism tries to keep us mindful of these ideas through symbols. These symbols are not new. They are the ones through which our fathers expressed the same ideas for centuries. As Jews, we perform the ceremonies and use the symbols of our people as they have been commanded to us and as they have developed among us. We find pleasure and take pride in conforming to them. It is not a mark of

THE THREE PILLARS

intellectual or ethical superiority for a Jew to ignore the customs and ceremonies of the Jewish people. It bespeaks rather his ignorance of the significance of his people's time-honored traditions.

SYMBOLS IN RELIGIOUS LIFE

If signs and ceremonies are important in the social and the national life of a people, they are even more so in the life of the spirit. Through them we express our emotions and religious ideas. Through their observance, even if only formal, religious feelings are aroused, thought is directed to spiritual channels and a devotional tendency is created. To deprive a child of religious ceremonies is to deny it food for religious growth; to deprive an adult, is to close up a natural channel of self-expression and thwart religious development. That mind will find its emotional expression in other ways.

Judaism is rich in its ceremonial life. All its symbols are fraught with historic significance and ethical import. Particular symbols for specific occasions will be considered in their due order. The *Shofar*,[1] the *Matzoh*, the *Sukkah*, the *Lulav*, and in a more extensive sense the

---

[1] No attempt has been made to preserve uniformity in the transliteration of Hebrew words. While the Sephardic system is used generally, words that have gained currency in English books on Jewish subjects and in general usage have been retained in their familiar form.

Sabbath and the holidays are, in themselves, symbols of definite ideas that Judaism is trying to teach. In addition, however, these general observances are to be noted in the course of daily life the year round.

THE MEZUZAH

The Jewish home has a *Mezuzah* on its door-post. It is a small oblong case of wood or metal, which contains on a piece of parchment the first two paragraphs of the *Shema* "Hear, O Israel, The Lord our God, The Lord is One. And thou shalt love the Lord thy God with all thy heart, and with all thy soul, and with all thy might. And these words, which I command thee this day, shall be upon thy heart; and thou shalt teach them diligently unto thy children, and shalt talk of them when thou sittest in thy house, and when thou walkest by the way, and when thou liest down, and when thou risest up. And thou shalt bind them for a sign upon thy hand, and they shall be for frontlets between thine eyes. And thou shalt write them upon the door-posts of thy house, and upon thy gates." (Deuteronomy 6:4–9 and also 11:13–20). On one side of the case is a circular cut to reveal the word "*Shaddai*," Almighty. It is hung slanting with this side outward on the right-hand post of each door in the home. The *Mezuzah* on the door-post is *not* a charm to ward off evil or to bring good luck. It is a reminder that the

THE THREE PILLARS

Jew regards the home as a sacred institution under the protection of God. It speaks constantly to each member of the family that the unity, the peace and the sanctity of that home must be preserved. In these days, many view with alarm the rapid development of forces which threaten to disrupt the home. A practice which tends to impress its importance exercises a beneficent influence over each particular home and helps to mold the general attitude of the community toward this fundamental institution of society. Thus the message of the *Mezuzah* on the doorposts grows doubly eloquent today.

BERACHOT

There is a saying among the sages that the Creator wishes man to enjoy all the good things that have been made for him, and that He will one day call to account those who, for no valid reason, deny themselves the legitimate pleasures of life. However, this enjoyment must be accompanied by a sense of gratitude. It is in this spirit of appreciative enjoyment — "To eat and to bless the Lord, for the good which He hath given thee," as the Torah has it, that the *Berachot* (blessings) have been in use in Jewish homes for centuries. Following are some of the blessings for food and fruits.

THE YEAR ROUND

On breaking bread: (*Ha-Motzi*)

בָּרוּךְ אַתָּה יְיָ אֱלֹהֵינוּ מֶלֶךְ הָעוֹלָם הַמּוֹצִיא לֶחֶם מִן הָאָרֶץ:

Boruch atto Adonoi Elohenu melech ho'olom, hamotzi lechem min ho'oretz.[1]

Blessed art Thou, O Lord our God, King of the universe, who bringest forth bread from the earth.

For wine:

בָּרוּךְ אַתָּה יְיָ אֱלֹהֵינוּ מֶלֶךְ הָעוֹלָם בּוֹרֵא פְּרִי הַגָּפֶן:

Boruch atto Adonoi Elohenu melech ho'olom, borei p'ri hagofen.

Blessed art Thou, O Lord our God, King of the universe, who createst the fruit of the vine.

For fruit grown on trees:

בָּרוּךְ אַתָּה יְיָ אֱלֹהֵינוּ מֶלֶךְ הָעוֹלָם בּוֹרֵא פְּרִי הָעֵץ:

Boruch atto Adonoi Elohenu melech ho'olom, borei p'ri ho'eitz.

Blessed art Thou, O Lord our God, King of the universe, who createst the fruit of the tree.

---

[1] Transliterations are included in this book but are not recommended for regular use. At best, they are spurs to the study of Hebrew.

THE THREE PILLARS

For vegetables, herbs and fruit which grow on the ground:

בָּרוּךְ אַתָּה יְיָ אֱלֹהֵינוּ מֶלֶךְ הָעוֹלָם בּוֹרֵא פְּרִי הָאֲדָמָה:

Blessed art Thou, O Lord our God, King of the universe,
who createst the fruits of the earth.

For meat, fish, eggs, milk, cheese, and beverages, except wine:

בָּרוּךְ אַתָּה יְיָ אֱלֹהֵינוּ מֶלֶךְ הָעוֹלָם שֶׁהַכֹּל נִהְיָה בִּדְבָרוֹ:

Blessed art Thou, O Lord our God, King of the universe,
by whose word all things exist.

For food, other than bread, prepared from cereal flour:

בָּרוּךְ אַתָּה יְיָ אֱלֹהֵינוּ מֶלֶךְ הָעוֹלָם בּוֹרֵא מִינֵי מְזוֹנוֹת:

Blessed art Thou, O Lord our God, King of the universe,
who createst the various kinds of food.

Besides these blessings of gratitude for the produce of the earth, there are others expressing awe at the wonderful phenomena of nature, thanksgiving at escape from danger, gladness at good tidings, and submission to the divine will upon receiving sad news.

THE YEAR ROUND

On witnessing a thunderstorm:

בָּרוּךְ אַתָּה יְיָ אֱלֹהֵינוּ מֶלֶךְ הָעוֹלָם שֶׁכֹּחוֹ וּגְבוּרָתוֹ מָלֵא עוֹלָם:

Blessed art Thou, O Lord our God, King of the universe, whose power and might fill the universe.

For lightning:

בָּרוּךְ אַתָּה יְיָ אֱלֹהֵינוּ מֶלֶךְ הָעוֹלָם עֹשֶׂה מַעֲשֵׂה בְרֵאשִׁית:

Blessed art Thou, O Lord our God, King of the universe, who renewest the work of creation.

On beholding the rainbow:

בָּרוּךְ אַתָּה יְיָ אֱלֹהֵינוּ מֶלֶךְ הָעוֹלָם זוֹכֵר הַבְּרִית וְנֶאֱמָן בִּבְרִיתוֹ וְקַיָּם בְּמַאֲמָרוֹ:

Blessed art Thou, O Lord our God, King of the universe, who rememberest the covenant, art faithful to Thy covenant and keepest Thy promise.

At the sight of the sea:

בָּרוּךְ אַתָּה יְיָ אֱלֹהֵינוּ מֶלֶךְ הָעוֹלָם עֹשֶׂה אֶת־הַיָּם הַגָּדוֹל:

Blessed art Thou, O Lord our God, King of the universe, who hast made the great sea.

On beholding budding blossoms:

בָּרוּךְ אַתָּה יְיָ אֱלֹהֵינוּ מֶלֶךְ הָעוֹלָם שֶׁלֹּא חִסֵּר בְּעוֹלָמוֹ דָּבָר וּבָרָא בוֹ בְּרִיּוֹת טוֹבוֹת וְאִילָנוֹת טוֹבִים לְהַנּוֹת בָּהֶם בְּנֵי אָדָם:

> Blessed art Thou, O Lord our God, King of the universe, who hast made Thy world lacking in nought, but hast produced therein goodly creatures, and goodly trees, to give delight unto the children of men.

Persons returning in safety from a sea or air voyage or a hazardous trip by land, and persons recovering from serious illness recite the following benediction in the presence of the congregation when called to the Torah:

בָּרוּךְ אַתָּה יְיָ אֱלֹהֵינוּ מֶלֶךְ הָעוֹלָם הַגּוֹמֵל לְחַיָּבִים טוֹבוֹת שֶׁגְּמָלַנִי כָּל טוֹב:

> Blessed art Thou, O Lord our God, King of the universe, who vouchsafest benefits unto the undeserving, who hast also vouchsafed all good unto me.

This benediction is referred to as *Bentschen Gomel* (prayer for safety).

The congregation responds:

מִי שֶׁגְּמָלְךָ כָּל טוֹב הוּא יִגְמָלְךָ כָּל טוֹב סֶלָה:

> He who hath vouchsafed unto thee all good, may He vouchsafe unto thee all good, Selah.

THE YEAR ROUND

Upon hearing good news:

בָּרוּךְ אַתָּה יְיָ אֱלֹהֵינוּ מֶלֶךְ הָעוֹלָם הַטּוֹב וְהַמֵּטִיב:

Blessed art Thou, O Lord our God, King of the universe, who art good and dispensest good.

On hearing sad news:

בָּרוּךְ אַתָּה יְיָ אֱלֹהֵינוּ מֶלֶךְ הָעוֹלָם דַּיַּן הָאֱמֶת:

Blessed art Thou, O Lord our God, King of the universe, the true Judge.

GRACE AT MEALS

From the Jewish point of view, a meal is more than the consuming of necessary food. It is elevated even above the genteel art of dining. It partakes of the nature of a sacrifice and is vested with an element of holiness. Indeed, the Rabbis say that a meal at which God's name is mentioned becomes a sacred function. Hence, Grace before and after meals has been instituted. This Grace serves as a reminder to the Jew that he does not live to eat, but eats to live, and to live for very definite exalted purposes. The recitation of Grace cannot fail to teach appreciation for the satisfaction of personal needs, sympathy for the larger family of humanity bound together by common wants, and gratitude to Him "who bringeth forth bread from the earth" for all.

THE THREE PILLARS

WASHING THE HANDS

The Grace before meals is preceded by the washing of the hands. The value of such a practice, teaching that cleanliness is not only next to godliness, but must precede it, is too obvious to need comment. Probably all children are urged to wash their hands before meals; adults do it as a matter of course. Judaism elevates this practice to the dignity of a religious ceremony by instituting a special blessing for this act.

בָּרוּךְ אַתָּה יְיָ אֱלֹהֵינוּ מֶלֶךְ הָעוֹלָם אֲשֶׁר קִדְּשָׁנוּ
בְּמִצְוֹתָיו וְצִוָּנוּ עַל נְטִילַת יָדָיִם:

Blessed art Thou, O Lord our God, King of the universe, who hast sanctified us by Thy commandments, and hast commanded us concerning the washing of the hands.

ARBA KANFOT

The *Arba Kanfot* with its four fringed corners (*Tsitsit*) has been described as the "uniform" of the Jew. The directions for making this garment are contained in the Bible: "And the Lord spoke unto Moses, saying: Speak unto the children of Israel, and bid them that they make them throughout their generations fringes in the corners of their garments, and that they put with the fringe of each corner a thread of blue." (Numbers 15:37-39.)

THE YEAR ROUND

The purpose of this garment is clearly given in the commandment which ordains it, "To look upon, to remember and to do, all the commandments of the Lord." The symbol of the *Tsitsit* then, is to serve as a reminder of specific things, as a constant incentive to nobility of conduct. The *Tsitsit* were originally attached to the outer clothing where they could be seen readily by wearer and observer alike. However, at one of those periods in Jewish history, when it meant death to be known as a Jew, the Rabbis agreed that a special garment (*Arba Kanfot*) with the *Tsitsit* might be worn underneath the outer clothing, so that the Jew could at least "remember" if not "look" upon them. Hence this institution now takes two forms — for purposes of worship, public or private, the *Tsitsit* becomes the fringed scarf known as the *Tallit*. This is worn over the outer clothing during prayer. But observant Jews wear throughout the day the *Arba Kanfot* or *Tallit Katon*.

SEPARATION OF THE DOUGH

The bread that is baked in a Jewish home is first consecrated. Such consecration of the dough, or the "taking of the *Ḥallah*," is closely connected with the tithe of Biblical origin. Tithing or giving of one's possessions as a tax or sacrifice, was a very ancient custom existing as early as the time of the Patriarchs and was made obligatory by the Mosaic Code. It is

THE THREE PILLARS

assumed that all our possessions are the Lord's and therefore to be consecrated to His service. Since we are in need of our possessions however, the dedication of part of them releases the remainder for our own uses. When making dough consisting of wheat, barley, oats, rye, a bit the size of a small egg is separated from the whole mass, if more than three pounds of flour are used. If there are two or more kinds of dough in preparation a small piece of each, to make the required amount must be separated. Previous to separating the dough, the following benediction is pronounced:

בָּרוּךְ אַתָּה יְיָ אֱלֹהֵינוּ מֶלֶךְ הָעוֹלָם אֲשֶׁר קִדְּשָׁנוּ
בְּמִצְוֹתָיו וְצִוָּנוּ לְהַפְרִישׁ חַלָּה:

Blessed art Thou, O Lord our God, King of the universe, who hast sanctified us by Thy commandments, and commanded us concerning the separation of the dough.

After the blessing the bit of dough is thrown into the fire or allowed to bake in the oven until quite burnt.

THE FUNDAMENTAL DUTIES OF THE JEWISH WOMAN

This "taking of the *Ḥallah*" together with the kindling of Sabbath lights and the observation of the purity laws (*Niddah*) constitute the three fundamental duties of the Jewish woman. They are particularly specified in Jewish Law. Their importance becomes evident in the light of their symbolism. The kindling of spiritual light, the consecration of our daily bread and the attainment of personal holiness — these are the lessons the Jewish woman has learnt so well from the observance of their outward expression in Jewish ceremony and practice. For a better understanding of her fundamental duties, it is essential that the Jewish woman participate in the institutes of adult studies and in the study groups provided by her rabbi and community.

Chapter II

MILESTONES

BRIT MILAH

The Jewish people are known for the love and devotion they lavish upon their children. This devotion extends beyond their physical well-being and education. It is equally, perhaps chiefly, concerned with their position as future Jewish men and women — as the next generation in the history of an eternal people. To have the child grow up as a worthy member of the Jewish community is the fondest wish of every parent. To this end, the male child is initiated into the Jewish covenant, when on the eighth day after birth, he is circumcised. This minor surgical operation is widely recommended by physicians today, and is becoming more and more common among non-Jews on a purely hygienic basis. But from the Jewish point of view, it is a religious act, a dedication of the child and his seed after him, to the people of Israel, and is accompanied by an elaborate religious ceremony. It is a distinguishing mark of a distinctive people. The wish, "May we live to see his *Bar Mitzvah*," so often expressed by friends at a *Brit*

Milah, breathes the hope that the child will thrive and develop and devote himself in his riper years, to the cause of God and his people.

CHOICE OF A NAME

The boy is named at his *Brit Milah* and assumes his place in the Jewish fold. Perhaps a word here about the choice of a name may not be out of place. What a pity that Jewish parents should ignore the beautiful Hebrew names, so rich in associations, and select those that help to disguise the Jewish character of their bearer. It is hardly because they are unconscious of the dignity of "Moses" or "Isaac," for instance. These names are highly esteemed, as is shown by the fact that they are so frequently selected as the Hebrew name of the boy, the name to be used for the purpose of Hebrew record. But it seems to require a little courage to bear their English equivalent. A boy so named may be subject to petty annoyance from ignorant companions. So Moses is changed to Monroe, while Isaac appears as Irving; Samuel becomes Stanley and Miriam is called Marjorie. It would seem that only a Lincoln can afford to be called Abraham, or a president's wife be known as Abigail. There are innumerable fine Jewish names that apparently only the most cultured type of non-Jew can appreciate — such names for instance, as David, Saul, Joshua, Nathan, Jonathan, Phineas, Judah, or Asher.

And when it comes to girls, among others, Ruth, Judith, Esther, Leah, Hadassah, Rachel, and Sarah, are surely worthy of consideration. What a sad reflection on Jewish taste, that most of our fine Jewish names are used only by Gentiles.

The Rabbis have a tradition that because the Israelites in Egypt did not change their names, they were delivered from bondage. There is more than mere fancy in the sentiment. Self-respect is certainly an index of spiritual independence as well as the condition for respect from others. At least we might reverse the process and gather from the respect paid to our Hebrew names by others, a little esteem for them ourselves. In Israel today, it is customary to give children significant Hebrew names.

NAMING OF GIRLS

Girls are named at the synagogue on the first Sabbath after their arrival, when the father is called up to the Torah. Sometimes the naming is postponed until the mother is able to be present. Natural impulse has made it a custom for the mother to attend the synagogue, either at a regular service or privately, to offer her thanksgiving for the safe arrival of her little one. A special service has been arranged for the occasion, the chief element of which is the *Gomel* benediction (page 24).

MILESTONES

PIDYON HA-BEN

The first-born among the children of Israel, both of man and of beast, belonged to the Lord (Exodus 13:1–2). Hence the Israelites were in duty bound to dedicate their own first-born male to the Lord, that is, to devote him to His active service. However, Mosaic law ordained that the first-born might be formally redeemed or repurchased by a specified sum of money. This religious ceremony of the formal redemption of the first-born (*Pidyon Ha-Ben*) occurs when the boy is thirty-one days old. A *Kohen*, a descendant of Aaron, the priestly tribe, redeems the child officially, and receives as redemption money five shekels. The ceremony is omitted when the father is a *Kohen* or *Levi* or the mother a daughter of a *Kohen* or *Levi*.[1]

BAR MITZVAH

One of the high occasions in the life of a Jewish mother is the thirteenth birthday of her son. On the Hebrew date, the boy becomes *Bar Mitzvah* (son of the Commandment). The ceremony marks an epoch in her career as a mother and an epoch in the life of her child.

---

[1] *Our Baby* published by the National Women's League includes special pages suitable for framing to commemorate the *Brit*, *Pidyon Ha-Ben*, and naming of a girl.

THE THREE PILLARS

To the boy, it gives an opportunity to publicly declare his loyalty to the Jewish people; to confirm of his own free will the dedication made at his *Brit Milah*. To the mother, it is a milestone in her child's life. At that time she surveys her child objectively, appraises his physical and moral estate, and plans for his future. Surely, among these future plans, there should be provision for a more intensive Jewish training. The *Bar Mitzvah* celebration ought not to be a farewell function to Jewish education. It should mark the beginning of higher training. On *Bar Mitzvah* day, one does not suddenly "become a man," as so many *Bar Mitzvah* boys eloquently announce. From that day, the boy is counted as a member of the Jewish community and he should begin his more serious preparation to make himself count. Such preparation for full Jewish manhood involves, above all, Jewish knowledge, the acquisition of which should be encouraged and sponsored for many years after *Bar Mitzvah*.

MINYAN

Two new elements enter into the boy's life at *Bar Mitzvah* time; he is counted for *Minyan* and is required to put on *Tefillin*. The mother should see that these privileges assume their proper place in his daily routine. The knowledge that he actually counts to make up a *Minyan* (the minimum of ten men required for a congregation) can easily be used to stimulate regular attendance at services with the rest of the community.

TEFILLIN

The purpose of the *Tefillin* (phylacteries) is to make him mindful of his direct personal relation to his God and aware of himself as a Jew. These *Tefillin* are bound on the left arm and forehead, to indicate that the Jew's deeds, his mind and his emotions (left arm near the heart) must stand the test of justice and mercy. As the *Tefillin* are placed in position this Biblical verse is recited: "I will betroth thee unto Me in righteousness, and in justice, in loving kindness and in mercy. I will betroth thee unto Me in faithfulness, and thou shalt know the Lord." (Hosea 2:21–22.) The *Tefillin* contain the first two sections of the *Shema* and two other significant sections of the Torah (Exodus 13:1–10; Exodus 13:11–16; Deuteronomy 6:4–9; Deuteronomy 11:13–21). Part of *Bar Mitzvah* preparation should be instruction in the proper placing of the *Tefillin*. Indeed, one month before the *Bar Mitzvah*, the boy must begin to wear them daily, except on Sabbaths and Festivals, while reciting the morning prayers, a habit which should be continued throughout life and encouraged by every Jewish parent.

BAT MITZVAH

It has become an increasingly widespread custom for a girl, also, to assume an important obligation in the year before her thirteenth birthday. In Jewish law, girls become of age at twelve years and one day, maturing one year sooner than boys. A girl who has had a thorough Hebrew education is given the opportunity of chanting a portion of the *Haftarah* at a late Friday evening service, or at a Sabbath morning service.

Every effort to make the *Bar Mitzvah* or *Bat Mitzvah* memorable is worthy and commendable. Gifts and parties are desirable and appropriate. Through all the rejoicing, however, the consciousness that the occasion is a religious celebration should be paramount. It is a fine practice for parents and children to contribute to a worthy cause on this occasion, and to begin at once to translate into action some of the generous impulses and nobler sentiments that the celebration stirs in the heart of the boy or girl.

CONFIRMATION

The custom of confirming girls and boys is observed in some synagogues and temples. There seems to be no fixed time for confirming them, this depending upon local custom and the practice of the particular synagogue. Frequently, confirmation is not observed until the age of sixteen, as a further goal in extending Hebrew education.

Confirmation should be preceded by a period of preparation in the study of the essentials of Jewish faith and practice, and no girl or boy ought to be admitted to confirmation before passing an examination manifesting a knowledge of these essentials.

The importance of the woman in Jewish life cannot be overestimated, and an intelligent Jewish woman bespeaks a certain amount of Jewish training and education. The saying of the Rabbis that "an ignorant man cannot be a pious man" is just as applicable to women. No effort is too great to help impress the seriousness of this sacred occasion and to strengthen the high resolves that it calls forth.

MARRIAGE

According to Jewish teaching, marriage is both a duty and the highest privilege. It is regarded as the ideal state, divinely founded for the happiness of the individual and the well-being of society. Marriage is a holy act, performed with God as a witness. It is called in the Bible "a divine covenant" or the "covenant of God" (Proverbs 2:17) and is known as *Kiddushin* (consecration) which indicates its sacred character. From the Jewish point of view all discussions of the superiority of man over woman are superfluous. (Genesis 2:18.) Husband and wife are regarded as equals, each as a helpmate for the other, each serving as the necessary complement to form a perfect whole.

The position of the Jewish wife is enviable. It is not left to the whim of the husband to determine her status and her rights. There are laws governing their mutual relations down to the minutest detail. They are dictated by the utmost tenderness and refinement, revealing the reverent attitude toward womankind that is characteristic of a home- and family-loving people. These laws concern themselves with every aspect of their united lives, their physical well-being, domestic and legal status, social relations, and dower rights. The justice and ethical import of most of these laws are so evident that they speak for themselves and reflect glory on the people who accepted these laws so far advanced that to this day the world at large has been unable to improve upon them.

MARITAL LAWS

Perhaps the conditions governing the physical relations of man and wife require a word of comment. There are basic Jewish laws referring to the marital life which safeguard health.

The sense of holiness and sanctification which are emphasized in the marriage ceremony, is thus periodically renewed, strengthening the marital bond.

MILESTONES

References to the periodic separation or *Niddah* period, and to the ritual bath, *Tevilah*, may be found in many books, including *The Laws and Customs of Israel* by Gerald Friedlander, *The Ways of Her Household* by Harris M. Lazarus, and *Religious Duties of the Daughters of Israel* by A. E. Hirschowitz.

Chapter III

DIETARY LAWS

PURPOSE OF DIETARY LAWS

The Jewish dietary laws, which may have had a sanitary and humane origin, serve as a means of distinguishing the Jewish people from its neighbors. This distinction however, is not regarded as an end in itself. It is considered the necessary condition for the fulfillment of a high and exalted aim. The discipline which the dietary laws impose is intended to develop the moral tone and character of the individual Jew. This developed moral tone must serve as the chief characteristic of the Jewish people who are to be witnesses of the Eternal and a priest people among the nations. Hence, these dietary laws have a twofold purpose — to develop the inner spiritual and moral power of the Jew, and to make him a spiritual force in the midst of mankind.

Even if we look for no other purpose than the development of the latent spiritual powers of the individual Jew, the dietary laws are sufficiently justified. For through them, the Jewish character has been disciplined. Abstinence from foods permitted to others develops and strengthens self-mastery and control. The daily prepara-

DIETARY LAWS

tion of foods in a specific manner serves as a constant reminder of an exalted spiritual life. The separation of the clean from the unclean, physically, helps considerably in developing a feeling for the separation of the morally clean and unclean. On the whole, nothing has refined the Jewish character as much as the dietary laws.

No scale has as yet been invented which can weigh the moral value and the spiritual influence that physical symbols and observance have. But it may safely be asserted that the tenderness of the Jewish people, their intense humanitarian emotions, their determined will, their love of peace and horror of bloodshed, are due in some measure to the sensitiveness secured through their observance of the dietary laws. And to their observance too, may be attributed the greater immunity from certain diseases and the greater longevity which characterizes this people.

The Jewish dietary laws have not exhausted their usefulness, for the world is as much in need today as ever of their spiritual value. They can still develop Jewish character and ennoble it. They can still help to keep this people distinct and conscious of their mission to be "holy unto the Lord."

THE JEWISH WOMAN AND THE DIETARY LAWS

The dietary laws must find their first expression in the home, and the Jewish woman must be their exponent.

THE THREE PILLARS

The observance of these laws should be a matter of importance and peculiar pride to every mother who seeks for her family those moral values that their observance tends to produce. To neglect them is to ignore an effective aid in character building — to say nothing of their importance as a distinguishing mark of a special people. In a Jewish home, a perfectly prepared meal, daintily served is not enough. It may satisfy the physical desires and the esthetic sense, but to be perfect, it must be prepared in accordance with the Jewish dietary laws; it must be *Kosher*, so that the discipline thus involved and the associations aroused may help sustain the spirit also.

MEANING OF KOSHER

There are several laws laid down in the Torah for the selection and preparation of foods. Foods selected and prepared in accordance with these laws are termed *Kosher*. *Kosher* does not in itself mean clean, although cleanliness is an indispensable attribute of all *Kosher* food. *Kosher*, used in reference to food, means *ritually correct*, that is, in accordance with the laws of the Torah and of Jewish tradition. Thus *Kosher* meat is meat that comes from animals selected according to the specifications of the Torah and slaughtered in accordance with the merciful and sanitary methods long established by our authorities.

DIETARY LAWS

MEANING OF TEREFAH

The word commonly used in contrast to *Kosher* (fit for food, ritually correct) is *Terefah*, which has come to mean unfit for food, or not in accordance with Jewish ritual requirements. In its literal sense *Terefah* means "torn by wild beasts." Anything torn by a beast, or *Terefah*, was *unfit* for food. Usage has widened the meaning of the word to include all animals unfit for use, whether they died a natural death or were not killed in prescribed form or were torn by wild beasts or found to have been diseased.

Some animals are forbidden because they in themselves are considered repulsive and hence are called "an abomination," because they are beasts of prey, or because they breed in places and thrive upon foods that may contain germs of disease. Among fowls, the prohibition is limited to the twenty-four kinds named in the Bible, such as the vulture, eagle, raven, ostrich, owl and bat (Leviticus 11:13-19). Creeping things and insects as well as oysters, clams, lobsters, crabs, and other shell fish are likewise forbidden for one or more of these reasons.

The Bible stipulates two requirements in the selection of animals fit for food, called clean. They are "whatsoever parteth the hoof, and is wholly cloven-footed, and cheweth the cud among the beast, that ye may eat." (Leviticus 11:2) Fishes that have fins and scales are clean, others unclean.

KOSHERING OF MEAT

In killing of animals for the use of their meat every precaution is taken to avoid unnecessary pain to them. Scripture further strictly forbids the eating of blood of beast or fowl. Hence every effort is made to remove the blood from all meat. It is *koshered*, that is, made fit for food, in accordance with Jewish law and tradition. This is done by soaking the meat in cold water for half an hour, in a bowl used only for this purpose. The meat is then thoroughly covered with salt by generous sprinkling on all sides and in all folds, placed upon an inclined or perforated board and allowed to drain for one hour. It is then washed under cold running water. This process removes not only surface blood and adhesions, but drains much of the blood that may have coagulated in the veins. Steaks and chops need not be koshered if they are to be broiled. When the surface blood has been washed away in cold water, they should be lightly sprinkled with salt and placed over an open fire or flame. They need not be washed again. The juice that escapes in the process of broiling is *Terefah*, inasmuch as it is the juice of unkoshered meat. Chops and steaks intended for frying must be *koshered* like all other meat. Liver is not *koshered*. It is cut in several places to allow the blood to run out through the slits, washed under the faucet, sprinkled with salt and broiled over an open fire, not on a paper, but in direct contact with the flame. After the broiling, the liver must be washed in cold running water. It is then ready for any further preparation.

In preparing a fowl for *koshering*, the following precautions must be observed. (1) A fowl made imperfect by an abnormal growth, one having a defect such as a bruised wing, broken back or missing gall bladder, or one in which a needle, pin or other foreign object is found, *is subject to question* (*she'elah*).[1] Fortunately, most *Kosher* meat and fowl is so scientifically and hygienically prepared under ritual supervision before it reaches the consumer that the average housewife rarely is confronted with these problems. (2) The jugular vein, that is, the vein on the under side of the neck where the slaughtering was done, must be removed. Since the cut was made at a certain point in the vein, separating it in two, care should be taken to pull out both parts. (3) If the heart is to be used, the tips at both ends must be cut off, and it must be cut open and slit in a criss-cross fashion. (4) The lungs should be discarded, and the naily ends cut from the wings and the legs. The liver is prepared as the liver of other animals in the way described above.

---

[1] In any doubt or question on ritual observance, the local rabbi should be consulted.

THE THREE PILLARS

BLOODSPECKED EGGS

The precaution against the consuming of blood, or "the life" as it is called in Biblical language, extends even to eggs. A drop of blood found on either the yolk or the white of an egg is considered an indication that the process of hatching has already begun, and the egg, containing the active germ of life, is therefore forbidden.

SEPARATION OF MEAT AND MILK PRODUCTS

The Torah three times repeats the law, "Thou shalt not seethe a kid in its mother's milk." The threefold repetition is traditionally explained as indicating a threefold prohibition; that of boiling meat and milk together, that of eating such a mixture and that of deriving any benefit therefrom. The historic reason for its prohibition is probably that the kid seethed in its mother's milk or other milk was used as part of the idolatrous rites of the surrounding peoples. In addition, the verse mentioned seems to point to the duty of self-restraint, as if to indicate that one must not greedily devour the first ripe fruits or the young, immediately upon their birth. A thought must be given to the perpetuation of the species, and to the tenderness that is due the weak and helpless.

Upon the basis of this verse, "Thou shalt not seethe a kid in its mother's milk," rests the whole system of the

DIETARY LAWS

separation of meat and milk. No foods may be prepared with meat and milk products together, and they ought not to be served at the same time. After partaking of a meal at which meat is served, it is forbidden to eat milk food until a certain time has elapsed, usually from three to six hours, depending upon local traditional custom. There must be separate sets of dishes and kitchen utensils, different silver, linen and table service for both types of food. As bread is eaten with both milk and meat, it should not contain either milk or meat products, unless it is intended for such meals only and its special character is clearly indicated. Foods which contain neither meat nor milk products, such as fruit, eggs or fish, are called *Parvah* foods. Dishes used for *Parvah* foods only, are called *Parvah* dishes.

All fruits and vegetables should be cut open or inspected before use. Especially is this true of spinach, peas, and prunes, which may contain worms or other insects. The same rule applies to cereals.

Chapter IV

PRAYER

THE SACRIFICIAL SYSTEM

Man's idea of the nature of his deity has kept pace with the progress of his general civilization. Yet however primitive his conception may have been, in the heart of the earliest man there existed a yearning to know his deity, to communicate with him, to speak to him of fears and needs, to show him gratitude and to pay him homage.

It is only natural that the method of communion or the way in which man tried to approach his god, has kept pace with the development of his thought and conception of the nature of the godhead. One of the earliest methods of communication was through the offering of sacrifices. Indeed, it was the principal method of worship among ancient peoples. Judaism retained this method of communion with the Divine, but gave to it a new content. The basic idea of sacrifice in the heathen mind was that of enjoying earthly possessions with his god and winning his favor through social communion, as it were. The Jews, however, made use of sacrifice to emphasize various spiritual concepts. They utilized this method of communion or approach to call to their minds the idea of sin and the necessity for purification, to express the feeling of gratitude and the desire for spiritual peace. Hence there were sin-offerings and thanksgiving-offerings and peace-offerings. The idea that it conveyed was the principal purpose of the sacrifice, which in Judaism was never viewed as an end in itself. Indeed, the Prophets pointed this out repeatedly. They spoke in unmistakable terms against the sacrificial system when unaccompanied by uprightness and holiness of life.

> "Yea, though ye offer me burnt-offerings and your meal-offerings, I will not accept them;
> Neither will I regard the peace-offerings of your fat beasts.
> But let justice well up as waters,
> And righteousness as a mighty stream."
>
> (Amos 5:22, 24.)

> "To what purpose is the multitude of your sacrifices unto Me?
> Saith the Lord;
> Your hands are full of blood,
> Wash you, make you clean,
> Put away the evil of your doings
> From before Mine eyes,
> Cease to do evil;
> Learn to do well;
> Seek justice, relieve the oppressed,
> Judge the fatherless, plead for the widow."
>
> (Isaiah 1:11, 15–17.)[1]

---

[1] See also Jeremiah 7:21–23; Psalms 40:7, 50:7–13.

DEVELOPMENT OF THE PRAYER SERVICES

During the Babylonian Exile, after the destruction of the First Temple (586 B. C. E., i. e., Before the Common Era), when there was no longer Temple nor sacrificial system, the words of the Prophets returned with startling clearness. The idea that the essential part of the sacrifice was the contrite heart that accompanied it, penetrated more than ever into the mind of the people.

It is probable that organized prayer as an institution arose at this period of the exile. The synagogue as such, probably had its origin or gained fresh impetus during the restoration of the new commonwealth by Ezra and Nehemiah (450 B. C. E.). Once organized, it retained its hold upon the people and with the establishment of the new commonwealth, regular organized prayer developed side by side with the sacrificial system in the second Temple. When the second Temple was destroyed by Titus (70 C. E., i. e., Common Era), the sacrifices naturally ceased, leaving prayer as the one means of communication with God.

PARALLEL ORDER OF SACRIFICIAL AND PRAYER SERVICES

The prayer services were held at the time appointed for sacrifice, and in some cases were called after the name of the sacrifice. To this day the parallel arrangement has been preserved in the liturgy of the synagogue,

PRAYER

which shows evidence of its origin in Temple worship. The *Siddur*, or arrangement of the prayers of Israel, carries out this order. The regular services held in the synagogue today like the regular sacrifices which were offered in the Temple are:

1. *Shaḥarit*, the morning service — corresponding to the morning sacrifice.
2. *Minḥah*, the noon service — corresponding to the noon sacrifice.
3. *Ma'ariv*, the evening service — corresponding with the completion of the sacrifice of the noon offering and private sacrifices.
4. *Musaf*, the additional service — corresponding to the additional sacrifice offered on Sabbaths, New Moons and Festivals after the morning sacrifice.

PRIVATE PRAYER

Prayer is a part of Jewish life, as of all spiritual life. It has been said, "No man is so poor as he who calls in agony, 'O God!' and to whom neither the heaven above nor the heart within answers, 'Behold, God is here.'"

It is perhaps true, that in the matters of the spirit, all men are not created equal. Some people are prayerfully disposed. To them spontaneous prayer is easy and serves as a spiritual stimulant. Others are not inclined to be prayerful. They can not easily open the heart; they can not at will lose themselves in communion with an unseen though ever-present God. But there comes from each heart at some time or other spontaneous expressions of joy, impassioned calls for Divine help, expressions of gratitude, and wonder at the marvels of the universe. These are the truest prayers, the unpremeditated outpouring of the heart. However, such moments are infrequent for most people and the spiritual life of the average individual needs the stimulation which is obtained by regular periods of prayer, both private and communal. This habit of prayer, like all other habits, must be cultivated. "More things are wrought by prayer than this world dreams of," says Tennyson. There is no doubt that "the man who prays, receives from the God towards whom he fervently lifts himself, the power to defy fate, to conquer sin, misery and death."

No one can dispense with prayer altogether. Only "the fool sayeth in his heart, there is no God." As long as man exists, his spirit will yearn to come in contact with his Creator, and the medium of approach is prayer.

Prayers may be divided into private and communal, that is, those said alone, and those said with a congregation. There are but few formal, set prayers for private use; that is, few as compared with those designed for communal purposes. Each heart knows its own desires and can best phrase its own needs. The few prayers for private use found in the Prayer Book and special compilations are intended primarily as helpful forms of expression.

PRAYER

NECESSITY FOR COMMUNAL WORSHIP

The communal or synagogue prayers are formulated, organized and arranged in a definite liturgy — the *Siddur*, or Prayer Book for week-days and Sabbaths, the separate *Mahzorim* (Holiday Prayer Books) for the various festivals, the *Haggadah* (Narrative) for *Seder* evenings, the *Kinot* (Dirges) for Tisha b'Av, and the *Selihot* (Penitential Prayers) for the Penitential days. These prayers do not concern themselves with the private needs of any one individual. They are petitions for the whole house of Israel and for all mankind. Hence these communal prayers are always plural in number, not "I" but "We," "Thy people Israel," or more inclusive still, "The children of all flesh." They are characterized by a spirit of Jewish brotherhood and at the same time, of universalism. This is because Israel regards itself and its destiny as an instrument in God's divine hands for His beneficent purposes toward all men. Hence when the prayers of Israel are most national, they are also most universal. Thus "when from Zion shall go forth the law and the word of the Lord from Jerusalem," it shall go forth to all men, bringing peace and healing in its wake. God is implored to gather His people from all the corners of the earth, so that all may see and know that He is king indeed. "On that day shall the Lord be king over all the earth, on that day shall the Lord be One and His name one." In this way is the destiny of Israel linked with the spiritual fate of the nations, and its prayers elevated far above the local or tribal to a universal plane.

These traditional prayers are a powerful force for developing Jewish consciousness and loyalty. They are a fountain of strength from which the heart of the Jew will ever draw fresh faith and courage. They are alive with the spirit of the past; they express the hope of Israel's future and the vision of the spiritual future of all men. If worship be a sincere expression of the innermost longings of the soul, and not a mere formality, it is bound to produce in the worshipper, not only a sense of communion with the Infinite, but a sense of fellowship with Israel and the whole of mankind.

Such communal prayer, created and hallowed by centuries of usage, should form a part of every life. We must find at least one period in the week for worship with the community of Israel, with whom we hold a kinship in hopes and ideals as well as in blood. The synagogue with its prayers and aspirations is the most important institution in Jewish life today, devoted to the perpetuation of Israel as a distinctive people. Parents who absent themselves from the synagogue or do not encourage their children to attend, may as well reconcile themselves to the loss of all Jewish feeling as far as their children are concerned. It is usual to speak of the synagogue as a *stronghold* of Jewish life. But the synagogue is a stronghold of Judaism only when its *hold*

PRAYER

is *strong* upon the people. It can be a powerful influence for enthusiasm, loyalty and knowledge in the life of every Jew who will give it the opportunity. And who has the right to deny this opportunity to herself or her children?

THE SIDDUR

The *Siddur*, or Prayer Book, is a compilation of the prayers of Israel, primarily intended for week-days and Sabbath. These prayers have been composed by various authors at various times, in various places. In its barest outline, it contains, among other prayers, the morning, afternoon and evening service for week-days and Sabbath, the Grace, night prayers, blessings and psalms for various occasions. Two of the chief portions in the *Siddur* are the *Shema*, the declaration of Israel's faith, and the *Shemoneh Esreh*. The *Shemoneh Esreh* (eighteen) is so called because originally it consisted of eighteen paragraphs, each one of which constituted a separate prayer ending with a benediction. The first three and the last three paragraphs of the *Shemoneh Esreh* do not change. The intermediate ones are altered to fit the occasion — week-day, Sabbath and the various festivals. The *Shemoneh Esreh* is usually recited aloud by the *Ḥazan* (Cantor) after the congregation has recited it in silence.

GENERAL CONTENTS OF THE SIDDUR

The following is a meager outline of the various parts of the services in their present form.

The Morning Service

1. Introductory Benedictions
2. Selected psalms
3. Introduction to *Shema* (3 paragraphs)
4. *Shema*
5. Concluding Benedictions to the *Shema*
6. *Shemoneh Esreh*
7. Closing Service

On Sabbaths, Festivals and Rosh Ḥodesh (First Day of the Month), an additional *Amidah* or *Musaf* is added. *Hallel*,[1] in part or the whole, is recited on these occasions as well as on Ḥanukkah.

The Afternoon Service

1. Psalm 145
2. *Shemoneh Esreh*
3. Closing Service

---

[1] Special prayers and psalms of praise (Psalms 113–118).

PRAYER

The Evening Service

1. Introductory Benedictions to the *Shema*
2. *Shema*
3. Concluding Benedictions to the *Shema*
4. *Shemoneh Esreh*
5. Closing Service

Since the service at the synagogue is designed for instruction as well as prayer, a section is read from the Torah on Sabbaths, new moons, festivals, semi-holidays, and on Monday and Thursday mornings. These selections are so arranged that the reading of the Law is completed in the course of the year. The Torah is divided into fifty-four sections, called *Parashot* or *Sidrot*, one *Parashah* or *Sidrah* being read each week. The reading of the Torah selection is followed on Sabbaths and festivals by the reading of an extract from the Prophets (*Haftarah*), usually having some connection with the *Parashah*.

The service at the synagogue is punctuated at various points by the *Kaddish*, which is recited, not as a mourner's prayer, but in its true aspect of congregational sanctification.

MAḤZOR

The book containing the collection of prayers for the New Year or the Day of Atonement or any of the three festivals is called a *Mahzor*. Usually the prayers for the three festivals, Pesah, Shavuot and Sukkot are bound together. While these *Mahzorim* may vary slightly in different countries, depending upon local history and traditions, they are alike in all essentials. In order to follow a congregational service easily, one must have the *Mahzor* used in that community.

Chapter V

THE BIBLE

THE BOOK OF BOOKS

The Bible is the source book of the highest religious truth that we possess. It is the depository of our knowledge of religion, of God and His relations to man, as conceived by Israel.[1] Israel's conception of the Divine has influenced and molded the religious conception of a large part of the civilized world. The Bible or the Holy Scriptures has been translated into almost every known language and dialect; it has been accorded the homage and veneration of millions of Jews and non-Jews the world over. The influence of no other book has been so great. It is indeed a unique book in the world, so unique, that it is called the "Book of Books," or the Bible, that is, *The Book*.

STRUCTURE OF THE BIBLE

In form, the Bible is divided into three parts. The first part is known as the *Torah* (the Law), as the *Ḥumash*

---

[1] Morris Joseph: *Judaism as Creed and Life*, Chapter II.

(the Five Books of Moses), or as the *Pentateuch*, which in Greek means fivefold. The books of the Torah are Genesis, Exodus, Leviticus, Numbers, Deuteronomy.

The second part of the Bible is known as the *Prophets*. This section divides itself into two parts, the first part called the *Earlier Prophets*, distinguished by the historical character of the books, which relate the events that occurred during the lives of the Earlier Prophets and which contain less of actual prophecy than of narrative. This section of the *Earlier Prophets* is composed of Joshua, Judges, the two books of Samuel and the two books of Kings. The second part is called the *Later Prophets*. These books are exhortatory in character, rather than historical, and the actual words of the Prophets are given, their exhortations and threats, their pleadings and consolations. This section consists of Isaiah, Jeremiah, Ezekiel, Hosea, Joel, Amos, Obadiah, Jonah, Nahum, Micah, Habakkuk, Zephaniah, Haggai, Zechariah, Malachi.

The third division of the Bible known as the *Hagiographa* is composed of the Psalms, Proverbs, Job, Canticles, Ruth, Lamentations, Ecclesiastes, Esther, Daniel, Ezra, Nehemiah and the two Books of Chronicles.

Sometimes, in a general sense the whole Bible is included in the term *Torah*. Since the Torah is the first and most important part of the Bible, the word is often used to designate the whole. Indeed, the term Torah, in an even more general sense, is taken to include, not only the whole Bible, but also the various commentaries and interpretations that have become traditional.

THE BIBLE AND TRADITION

In the eagerness of the Jew to understand his Bible and apply its principles in his daily life, every word contained therein became the subject of reverent and loving interpretation. Especially is this true in the case of the Torah, whose every dot and letter was vested with deep meaning. The whole system of Jewish tradition and of all Rabbinic legislation is grounded solely and solidly on the basis of the Torah. It has been said that as soon as the Torah was given, Jewish scholarship began. Hence there is the statement, in a more general sense, that not only the *written law*, but also the *oral law* was revealed at Sinai; that is, not only is the Torah law itself holy and binding, but those interpretations and applications that have been developed from it are also holy and binding, since they are inherent in the nature of the Torah and in its very essence.

The profound ethical principles of the Bible, which remain eternally true, its sublimity and spiritual elevation, distinguish it as the work of men of extraordinary spiritual vision; men, who through some special endowment seemed to have been able to approach closely the Divine Spirit and to have been kindled with His holy fire.

"INSPIRATION" DEFINED

When we say that the Bible is "inspired" we mean to convey the idea that the relation of God to the men who wrote it was of a peculiar nature, different from His relation towards other men, and that the activity of these men was originated and directed by God's special will toward them. It is to this perfect adjustment of their very being towards God that we refer, when we say of the Prophets and authors that they were inspired. Especially is this true in the case of Moses, who "saw God face to face," whose relations to God must have been unique indeed. Hence we speak of the Law being *revealed* through Moses, conceiving of Moses as a perfect medium for the expression of the Divine Will. It seems as if God indeed breathed of His spirit into these men and they became transformed. In Bible language, "the spirit of the Lord rested upon them, and they prophesied."

FORMATION OF THE CANON

The Bible is a compilation of many books by many authors. Some of these books bear their author's name, like Joshua, Isaiah, Jeremiah and Zechariah. Some derive their names from the author of the first part of the contents, as for example, Samuel, and some from the general contents of the book itself — Ruth, Song of Songs. Others are called in Hebrew by the first characteristic word, as for instance, all the books of the Torah.

The Torah, in its limited sense as the five books of Moses, is the heart of the Hebrew Bible. The Bible in its present form is the result of consecutive additions to this Torah nucleus covering a period of many centuries. From the vast amount of sacred Hebrew literature extant, selected books were added to the Torah during various periods in Jewish history. These books were the ones which seemed to teach best, valuable religious doctrine and which had been generally adopted for public reading because of their inspired character. There came a period in Jewish life when the scholars and leaders felt that the Torah and those inspired writings which had been added gradually to it comprised a perfect whole, unified in spirit. They decided to combine these literary treasures into an official sacred collection. It was feared that unless this was done these works might be lost or even altered. This collection, in its final form, as we have it now, is our Bible.

APOCRYPHA

There were many books in use not included in the official collection, or Bible, for some cause or other. However, it was commonly felt that they, too, contained a certain religious and inspirational value. These books were also collected and are called the *Apocrypha*, which means "writings away from" or "hidden," because they were for the time being, actually kept from sacred use, in order to throw the emphasis upon the official Canon. Among these are now the Books of the Maccabees, Judith, Tobit, Ecclesiasticus or the Wisdom of Ben Sira.

THE BIBLE AND THE CHOSEN PEOPLE

There is no country in the western world where the Bible is not held in veneration, where its teachings are not acknowledged as the highest ethical concepts. The Ten Commandments, the prophecies of Isaiah, the Psalms of David, have not yet been surpassed or equalled. Yet of all peoples, it is upon the Jews in particular that the Bible has a claim for reverence and love. Its setting is the land of the Jew, its coloring is Jewish, its characters are Jews, it contains the history of the Jewish people, beginning with the first Patriarch and covering a period of over a thousand years. It is the chronicle of Jewish events, penned by inspired historians. It is the national history of a people and as such is entitled to the place which is accorded all national annals. Considered as a part of Jewish literature, the Bible elevates the people that could produce it to a unique position. In it also, Israel will find its commission from God, the charter, as it were, of its peculiar destiny. "Ye are My witnesses," saith the Lord. "Ye shall be holy unto Me." "And ye shall be My people and I will be your God."

THE BIBLE

In it, the Jew hears, like Isaiah in his vision, the voice of God asking, "Whom shall I send?" And it contains the answer of Isaiah and the Jew, "Send me." The words of the multitude as they accepted the Law, "We will obey and we will harken," sealed their commission as a priestly people among the nations.

SYSTEMATIC STUDY OF THE BIBLE

It is a mark of gross ignorance for anyone to be unfamiliar with the Bible; for a Jew to be ignorant of his Bible is nothing short of a tragedy. It is *his* canon or rule of life. It is the record of *his* history.[1] It is *his* literature. Familiarity with the Bible is not only a part of culture in general; it is a part of Judaism in particular. There should be a Bible in every Jewish home and it should be there for use, not as an accepted addition to the furnishings, or because it is deemed the proper thing to have one on a small table between two bookends.

The purpose of the Bible is to serve as a moral teacher and guide. This is so widely recognized that outside of religious circles, in purely secular institutions, in schools and colleges, an effort is made to give students some familiarity with the Bible by reading selections at assemblies and in classrooms. The selections, however, are not always satisfactory, and they are necessarily

---

[1] Morris Joseph: *Judaism as Creed and Life*, Chapter II.

brief. Better acquaintance with the Bible is secured by following the reading of the Torah and the Prophets at synagogue services on the Sabbath and holidays. The cycle of a year will cover the whole Torah or Pentateuch and fifty-two selected prophetic passages. Indeed, that is what the public reading is for — to acquaint the congregation with the Bible. But even this synagogue instruction should be supplemented by the systematic reading of a chapter a day.

It should not be necessary to marshal arguments for Bible reading, or to point out that not only Jews, but all great men have found in it their chief source of inspiration, — that for instance, Abraham Lincoln knew his Bible thoroughly, or that the poets and classic English authors abound in Biblical reference. Our fathers so loved this great Book that they meditated on it day and night. The influence of the Book on their character and life was incalculable. Our ignorance is the result of neglect. Theoretically we are all agreed that we ought to study the Bible, but we seldom put this theory into practice. A few minutes a day, every day, would soon make one acquainted with the greatest Book in the world.

Chapter VI

THE SABBATH

IMPORTANCE OF THE SABBATH IN JEWISH LIFE

The value of a periodic day of rest is now generally admitted. It influences the physical well-being of the individual and his attitude toward his work. It gives him an opportunity for physical rest and for communion with his higher self, which the toilsome week denies him. However, this principle of a regular rest-day now so widely recognized, was once unknown. The people of Israel, who first dared to proclaim and practice it, were made the object of ridicule and abuse. They were accused of being idlers and of "making of their laziness, a religion," as the Latin writer Juvenal puts it.

The Sabbath has been and is the keystone of the entire structure of Jewish life. When that is removed, all the rest of Jewish life crumbles. It cannot be sustained by improvised props. No substitutes for the Sabbath have yet been found. The experience of modern Jewry in every part of the world proves that neglect of Sabbath consecration leads to indifference to other aspects of Jewish life and to the ties which hold us to religious duty. It is only a matter of time for this indifference to give way to intermarriage and apostasy. And it is equally true that the individual's observance of the Sabbath, together with the rest of the community, tends to produce a better understanding and a deeper sympathy with things Jewish, and to develop loyalty and appreciation, not only for the Sabbath ideal, but for kindred ideals in Judaism.[1] Our fathers regarded the day, with its peace and opportunity for spiritual regeneration, as a gift of God, a manifestation of His tenderness toward His children, and called it in reverence, "Queen Sabbath," and in love, the "Sabbath Bride."[2] History has proven that this attitude was correct. It has well been said that even more than Israel has kept the Sabbath, the Sabbath has kept Israel.

THE WOMAN'S PART IN ITS PRESERVATION

To the preservation of the Sabbath, the Jewish woman has contributed an important part. It was the mother in the home, whose eager preparations for the Sabbath created an atmosphere of happy expectation and left an indelible impress upon the members of her family Sabbath without the mother was almost inconceivable, and today, Sabbath without the mother is still more difficult. For in many homes it is she who must assume

---

[1] H. Pereira Mendes: *Jewish Daily Life*, p. 70 and ff.
[2] Solomon Schechter: *Studies in Judaism* I, p. 246 and ff.

THE SABBATH

almost the entire responsibility of fostering her children's religious life and of transmitting to them that spiritual heritage which has molded her own. Under modern conditions, it is the mother who becomes the guardian of the Sabbath and its interpreter. She can best fulfill this duty by observing the day in the traditional manner and utilizing every means to make it attractive to her children.

GENERAL PREPARATIONS

Marketing and cooking are prohibited on the Sabbath and therefore Friday, *Erev Shabbos*, is the day devoted to necessary preparations for the Sabbath. These include besides the cooking of the regular meals, and special Sabbath dishes, the provision of special table appointments, that is, the Sabbath lights, the loaves of Sabbath bread (*Ḥallas*), and the wine for *Kiddush*. These preparations cover also those innumerable household details which must be adjusted to create an atmosphere of Sabbath peace and leisure. Snowy linen, sparkling silver, flowers, Sabbath garb, the welcome friend and stranger, all contribute toward making the Sabbath the climax of the week. The true spirit of the day can best be caught in the home circle, and all the family ought to take part in its celebration. Every child should have some special little duty in its preparation. One cannot overestimate the effect on the child of so simple an act as the preparing of the Sabbath lights or the setting of the table, "for Shabbos."

THE SABBATH LIGHTS

The first formal welcome to the Sabbath is given by the mother of the home. To her is conceded the privilege of kindling the Sabbath lights, as a tribute to her influence in the family circle and through it, upon wider spheres. It is an effective custom to provide separate candles for the oldest daughter in the home to light. The memory of that practice and its associations will do much to insure her observance of the ceremony in mature life. The Sabbath lights must be kindled shortly before sunset. The following benediction is pronounced after the lights have been kindled.

בָּרוּךְ אַתָּה יְיָ אֱלֹהֵינוּ מֶלֶךְ הָעוֹלָם אֲשֶׁר קִדְּשָׁנוּ
בְּמִצְוֹתָיו וְצִוָּנוּ לְהַדְלִיק נֵר שֶׁל שַׁבָּת:

Boruch atto Adonoi, Elohenu melech ho'olom, asher kidshonu b'mitzvosov, v'tzivonu l'hadlik nair shel shabbos.

Blessed art Thou, O Lord our God, King of the universe, who hast sanctified us by Thy commandments, and commanded us to kindle the Sabbath lights.

Regular services are held at the synagogues at sundown[1] to greet the Sabbath with appropriate prayer

---

[1] The Jewish day begins at sundown.

and praise. One of the Sabbath eve prayers is the special greeting to the Sabbath, the *"Lecho Dodi"* — "Come, my beloved, the Bride to greet." If attendance at synagogue is impossible, a family service should be held at home after the kindling of the lights. There are several arrangements of Friday evening services, providing responsive reading and singing in which all can join.

BLESSING THE CHILDREN

A beautiful Jewish custom on the Sabbath is the blessing of the children by the parents, either after lighting the Sabbath candles or before the recital of the *Kiddush*. The parents, placing their hands on the bowed heads of the children in turn, invoke God's blessing upon them, saying to the boys:

יְשִׂימְךָ אֱלֹהִים כְּאֶפְרַיִם וְכִמְנַשֶּׁה:

Yesimcho Elohim k'Ephrayim vechi-Menasheh

God make thee as Ephraim and as Manasseh.

and to the girls:

יְשִׂימֵךְ אֱלֹהִים כְּשָׂרָה רִבְקָה רָחֵל וְלֵאָה:

Yesimech Elohim k'Soroh Rivkoh Roḥel v'Leah.

God make thee as Sarah, Rebekah, Rachel and Leah.

"It is at such moments that parents best realize the holiness of parenthood, and children the holiness of filial reverence."[1] And it is only natural that children reared in such an atmosphere should carry into their daily life those intangible but potent influences that make for noble Jewish manhood and womanhood.

KIDDUSH

The ceremony of *Kiddush* or Sanctification was instituted as a means of fulfilling the first part of the fourth commandment, which reads, "Remember the Sabbath day to keep it holy." It thus becomes the duty of every Jew to be conscious of the holiness of the Sabbath day, as soon as it begins on Friday evening at sunset. This is done at the synagogue by special services and *Kiddush*.[2] At home, the father or an honored guest usually recites the *Kiddush*. In the absence of any male, this is done by the mother.[3] Those present follow the reader as he acknowledges God the Creator of all, thanks Him for the Sabbath rest, recalls His mercy to His people, and Israel's duty to observe the day. The cup of sanctification is then partaken of by all present. After the washing

---

[1] H. Pereira Mendes: *Jewish Daily Life*, p. 73 and ff.

[2] The *Kiddush* is primarily a home ceremony. It was added to the synagogue service during the period when living facilities were attached to the house of worship for the homeless and those away from home who might otherwise not have had the privilege of hearing the *Kiddush* recited.

[3] The same applies to the *Havdalah*.

THE SABBATH

of the hands (page 26), the Sabbath loaves are broken with the following benediction:

בָּרוּךְ אַתָּה יְיָ אֱלֹהֵינוּ מֶלֶךְ הָעוֹלָם הַמּוֹצִיא לֶחֶם מִן הָאָרֶץ׃

Boruch atto Adonoi, Elohenu melech ho'olom, hamotzi lechem min ho'oretz.

Blessed art Thou, O Lord our God, King of the universe, who bringest forth bread from the earth.

These two loaves of Sabbath bread are symbolic, among other things, of the twofold commandment given to Israel to keep the Sabbath,[1] and of the double portion of manna supplied the Israelites for the Sabbaths in the wilderness.

GRACE AFTER MEALS AND ZEMIROT

The Sabbath meal is followed by Grace, which should be recited by the whole family and which has ample provision for chanting and responses. The *Zemirot*, beautiful traditional melodies of praise, hallowed by centuries of usage, are usually sung during the meal. They can best be learned by the new generation and preserved in this manner.

---

[1] "Remember the Sabbath Day to Keep it Holy" (Exodus 20:8). "Observe the Sabbath Day to Keep it Holy" (Deuteronomy 5:12).

In many modern congregations, additional services are held on Friday evening at about eight o'clock. These services are intended to afford an opportunity for synagogue worship to those who have not attended the traditional *Kabbalat Shabbat* service at sunset. The exact time, duration and character of these special services are determined by the leaders in the respective congregations. These services usually consist of congregational singing, responsive reading and a sermon.

SABBATH MORNING SERVICES

Nothing ought be permitted to stand in the way of regular attendance at services on Sabbath morning. Participation in community worship is the main point of contact between the individual Jew and his people. This contact serves as a means of transmitting Israel's hopes and ideals and as an inspiration toward their fulfillment. Regular attendance at the synagogue is a habit that should begin in childhood and be strengthened not by precept alone but by example on the part of the parents. Individual Prayer Books with a good English translation and an explanation of the order of the services are essential for all public worship.

GENERAL OBSERVANCE OF DAY

The general arrangement of the day should be determined by a proper sense of its true character and purpose. It is, first of all, a day of rest, a day to be marked by the cessation of the weekly round of work. Yet not rest only, but rest sanctified by spiritual endeavor is the Sabbath ideal. Our Rabbis insist so strenuously upon the duty of resting that they take the utmost pains to define what constitutes work, including among other things, baking, cooking, sewing, writing, kindling and extinguishing fires, tearing, cutting — in all, thirty-nine categories of labor. To keep the Sabbath properly, one must devote some part of the day to religious exercises, to prayer, meditation, and to some serious study, as well as to those kinds of physical enjoyment which make the day bright and lovable, while not interfering with its repose. Obviously, exciting games, struggling in noisy, hurrying crowds, theatres, card parties, and similar gatherings, are not consistent with the Sabbath spirit, while marketing, shopping and manual labor are a direct violation of the Sabbath law. Recreation on the Sabbath day is not merely permissible; it is a duty. But it is a duty that must not be fulfilled at too high a price. Its fulfillment must be subordinated to the spirit of the day.

HAVDALAH

The *Kiddush* on Friday evening constitutes a formal welcome to the Sabbath. The *Havdalah* just after nightfall on Saturday, marks its close. This ceremony of

THE THREE PILLARS

Havdalah or "separation" designates the point between the end of the Sabbath of rest and the beginning of the week of labor. Blessings are recited over wine, spices and a candle flame, calling into play the senses of taste, smell and touch, which, together with the symbols that we see and the benedictions that we hear, constitute our five senses and are our best equipment for the week's work. The service reminds us that these faculties must be used only in ways that are acceptable in the eyes of God.

CHAPTER VII

ROSH HA-SHANAH — NEW YEAR

GENERAL CHARACTER OF THE SEASON

The first ten days of the seventh month, Tishri, form a period different in character from the cycle of the three festivals, Pesaḥ, Shavuot and Sukkot.[1] They have no agricultural origin, and they do not commemorate any historical event in the life of Israel. They concern themselves with such questions as the meaning of life, moral effort and the human conscience; sin, repentance and spiritual regeneration; in short, they deal with the reality and value of the spiritual life. There is nothing tribal or temporal in these questions. They appeal to the human rather than to the Jewish side of our nature. These subjects suggest themselves to all thinking men and are thus of a most universal character. Yet they touch each man and his own conscience so that they are particular and individual as well.

---

[1] Morris Joseph: *Judaism as Creed and Life*, p. 247 and ff.

THE THREE PILLARS

ASERET YEMAI TESHUVAH

The keynote of the whole season is *Teshuvah*, Return or Repentance. It is assumed that man is fundamentally good and desires to do the right; that his sins have been committed through weakness in wandering from the right path. At this season, he is especially urged to return to the proper path of conduct, assured of forgiveness and mercy if he will but recognize the error of his ways, rectify as far as is humanly possible his evil deeds, and determine to sin no more. The season makes an appeal to each individual to strive for the highest religious and moral life of which he is capable.

Thus these *Yomim Noroim* provide for the periodic regeneration of the Jewish People. They form the great annual revival period, the time when the sublime teachings of the Torah and prophets are brought into striking relief against the drab background of indifferent daily existence; the time when the spiritual heights to which man may attain are revealed as the goal for his strivings.

YOMIM NOROIM

The first two days of Tishri are Rosh Ha-Shanah, the New Year. The tenth day is Yom Kippur, the Day of Atonement. These three days, filled as they are with awesome thoughts, are called the *Yomim Noroim*, the Days of Awe. These *Yomim Noroim* together with the intervening days form the *Aseret Yemai Teshuvah*, the Ten Days of Penitence.

The whole period of the *Yomim Noroim* is regarded of such importance that it is preceded by a season of special spiritual preparation. Beginning with the Sunday before Rosh Ha-Shanah or two Sundays before, special penitential prayers at midnight (*Seliḥot*) are added to the regular morning service at the synagogue and the *Shofar* is blown daily. It is customary also to visit the graves of one's parents during this month, to reflect upon their instructions and teachings and to gather fresh inspiration for their fulfillment.

THE TWO NEW YEARS

The Israelites dated a new period in time with the birth of their physical freedom, and called Nisan, the month in which Passover came, the first month, or the head of the months. Hence the first day of Nisan is the national New Year. But the Jew lives by the spirit also and Rosh Ha-Shanah, the time that should mark the new life of the spirit, begins the religious New Year for this people. It is at this season and not at Nisan that the calendar New Year is dated.

THE THREE PILLARS

ROSH HA-SHANAH AS YOM TERUAH

Rosh Ha-Shanah is known by several names, each emphasizing an aspect of the holy day. It is called, primarily, *Yom Teruah*, the Day of the Blowing, from the distinctive ceremony, the blowing of the *Shofar*.

The *Shofar* carries with it many associations. It is, first of all, made of a ram's horn, recalling the *Akedah*, or sacrifice of Isaac (Genesis 20), the sublimest example of faith and obedience in all history. Repeated reference to this incident occurs in the prayers of the day. The *Shofar* was used in Palestine to announce the new moon, the Sabbath, the Jubilee and other momentous occasions, and its sound is intended to arouse the heart to the solemnity of Rosh Ha-Shanah. It also was used to assemble the hosts of Israel when they were encamped in the wilderness and to sound the alarm for battle, and seems to call upon those who hear it to muster all moral forces for this annual attempt to assert the supremacy of the spirit. The *Shofar* is further associated with God's revelation at Mount Sinai, and Israel's willingness to assume the responsibilities of the Law. Tradition connects it, too, with the final revelation of God to all mankind and thus its message of hope is not confined to the Jewish people, but is universal in its reach.

ROSH HA-SHANAH — NEW YEAR

ROSH HA-SHANAH AS YOM HA-ZIKORON

Rosh Ha-Shanah is known as *Yom Ha-Zikoron*, the Day of Memorial. According to tradition, Rosh Ha-Shanah is the birthday of the world and at this season each year, "everything is remembered from the beginning." As the passage in the special service has it, "Thou rememberest what was wrought from eternity, and art mindful of all that hath been formed from of old; before Thee all secrets are revealed and the multitude of hidden things from the beginning, for there is no forgetfulness before the throne of Thy glory; nor is there aught hidden from Thine eyes."

ROSH HA-SHANAH AS YOM HA-DIN

The purpose of this memorial is explicitly stated. It is the time when God judges all created things and provides for their needs according to their merits. Not only Israel is provided for at this season, but there is no creature that breathes, which is forgotten. "For Thou wilt bring on the appointed time of memorial, when every spirit and soul shall be visited ... Thereon sentence is pronounced upon countries ... and every creature is visited thereon and recorded for life or for death. For the remembrance of every creature cometh before Thee, man's deeds and destiny, his works and ways, his thoughts and schemes, his imaginings and achievements ... and Thou enquirest into the doings of them all."

Perhaps this aspect of Rosh Ha-Shanah as the *Yom Ha-Din*, the Day of Judgment, requires a word of explanation. The Jew is perfectly conscious that he is judged every moment of his life and that his every thought and deed determine his fate. Yet these *Yomim Noroim* are selected as the time to impress this truth upon his mind and are conceived as a season of special mercy, when God is particularly near and ready to forgive. In the words of the prophet Isaiah:

> "Seek ye the Lord while He may be found.
> Call ye upon Him while He is near;
> Let the wicked forsake his way,
> And the man of iniquity his thoughts;
> And let him return unto the Lord,
> And He will have compassion upon him,
> And to our God, for He will abundantly pardon."
> (Isaiah 50: 6.)

It is a time when mercy not only tempers justice, but far outweighs it. And Rosh Ha-Shanah is the Day of Judgment in a second sense, a time devoted to introspection and impartial self-criticism.

ROSH HA-SHANAH AS THE NEW YEAR

It is only the individual who can make Rosh Ha-Shanah a New Year for himself. Hence the figurative saying of the Rabbis that God himself cannot proclaim the Rosh

ROSH HA-SHANAH — NEW YEAR

Ha-Shanah in heaven until Israel has done so on earth. The freshened vision of what Jewish life should be, inculcates the desire to make another start, to begin anew. Hence the name *New Year* — the time for a new birth in the life of the spirit.

SYNAGOGUE SERVICES

There are evening, morning and afternoon services for both days at all the synagogues. It is absolutely essential to have the special Prayer Book (*Mahzor*) used in the particular synagogue, from which to follow the services at these times. Many of the passages are of such sublimity and inspiration that the mere reading of them cannot fail to ennoble. The *Shofar* is sounded several times during the services. Even when for personal reasons it is impossible to remain during the whole morning service, a partial attendance, covering the time of the *Shofar* blowing ought to be arranged for. Indeed, it is forbidden to partake of any food before hearing the *Shofar* call on Rosh Ha-Shanah mornings, unless this causes positive illness or distress.

BOOK OF LIFE

The prayer, "Inscribe us in the Book of Life," occurs repeatedly during the service. This is associated with the conception of the Sages, that there are opened

THE THREE PILLARS

before the Great Judge at this season, three books — the Book of Life into which the righteous are immediately entered, the Book of Death for the irredeemably wicked, and the Book of Suspended Judgment, for the average person, whose conduct during the penitential days will decide his fate. "Penitence, prayer and charity may avert the evil decree." At *Neilah*, the concluding service of Yom Kippur, the last day of the *Aseret Yemai Teshuvah*, the expression is changed from "Inscribe," to "Seal us in the Book of Life," for at that time the final record is made.

It has become a custom to exchange greetings, good wishes and gifts for the New Year among relatives and friends, while in many homes Rosh Ha-Shanah is made the time of family reunions. Goodwill expressed in kind deeds comes spontaneously, for the heart is softened at this season and tender emotions are easily evoked.

SEASON'S GREETINGS

The proper greeting of the season, from the evening before Rosh Ha-Shanah is,

To an individual male	לְשָׁנָה טוֹבָה תִּכָּתֵב[1]
To more than one	לְשָׁנָה טוֹבָה תִּכָּתֵבוּ

---

[1] Transliteration for general use — "L'shonoh tovoh tikotevu."

ROSH HA-SHANAH — NEW YEAR

To an individual woman   לְשָׁנָה טוֹבָה תִּכָּתֵבִי

To more than one   לְשָׁנָה טוֹבָה תִּכָּתֵבְנָה

May you be inscribed for a happy year.

And its reply,

To men   גַּם אַתֶּם[1]

To women   גַּם אַתֶּן

The same to you.

ERUV TAVSHILIN

The permission to prepare food on the holidays is restricted to food required for these days. However, if the holiday is followed by the Sabbath or if the second day of the holiday falls on the Sabbath, the food for the Sabbath may be prepared on that holiday, provided such preparation has commenced before the festival. The first step of the preparation for the Sabbath to come is called *Eruv Tavshilin* — the link that unites the cooking and is performed shortly before the holiday begins. *Eruv Tavshilin* is performed by reciting the following formula over a small quantity of some cooked food, such as meat, fish or egg, together with some bread (*Matzoh* on Pesaḥ):

---

[1] Transliteration for general reply — "Gam atem."

THE THREE PILLARS

בָּרוּךְ אַתָּה יְיָ אֱלֹהֵינוּ מֶלֶךְ הָעוֹלָם אֲשֶׁר קִדְּשָׁנוּ בְּמִצְוֹתָיו וְצִוָּנוּ עַל מִצְוַת עֵרוּב:

Blessed art Thou, O Lord our God, King of the universe, who hast sanctified us by Thy commandments, and commanded us concerning the Eruv.

בַּהֲדֵין עֵרוּבָא יְהֵא שָׁרָא לָנָא לְמֵיפָא וּלְבַשָּׁלָא וּלְאַטְמָנָא וּלְאַדְלָקָא שְׁרָגָא וּלְמֶעְבַּד כָּל־צָרְכָּנָא מִיּוֹמָא טָבָא לְשַׁבַּתָּא לָנוּ וּלְכָל־הַדָּרִים בָּעִיר הַזֹּאת:

By virtue of this Eruv, be it permitted to us to bake, cook, keep food warm, kindle lights and do all the work that is necessary, on the festival, for the Sabbath, to us and to all the Israelites that dwell in this city.

Candles are lit, as for the Sabbath.

FESTIVAL LIGHTS

Blessing over the candles (page 70) on a week-day:

בָּרוּךְ אַתָּה יְיָ אֱלֹהֵינוּ מֶלֶךְ הָעוֹלָם אֲשֶׁר קִדְּשָׁנוּ בְּמִצְוֹתָיו וְצִוָּנוּ לְהַדְלִיק נֵר שֶׁל יוֹם טוֹב:

Boruch atto Adonoi, Elohenu melech ho'olom, asher kidshonu b'mitzvosov, v'tzivonu l'hadlik nair shel yom tov.

Blessed art Thou, O Lord our God, King of the universe, who hast sanctified us by Thy commandments, and commanded us to kindle the Festival lights.

ROSH HA-SHANAH — NEW YEAR

Blessing over the candles on a Friday night:

בָּרוּךְ אַתָּה יְיָ אֱלֹהֵינוּ מֶלֶךְ הָעוֹלָם אֲשֶׁר קִדְּשָׁנוּ בְּמִצְוֹתָיו וְצִוָּנוּ לְהַדְלִיק נֵר שֶׁל שַׁבָּת וְשֶׁל יוֹם טוֹב:

Boruch atto Adonoi, Elohenu melech ho'olom, asher kidshonu b'mitzvosov, v'tzivonu l'hadlik nair shel shabbos v'shel yom tov.

Blessed art Thou, O Lord our God, King of the universe, who hast sanctified us by Thy commandments, and commanded us to kindle the Sabbath and Festival lights.

Add each night:

בָּרוּךְ אַתָּה יְיָ אֱלֹהֵינוּ מֶלֶךְ הָעוֹלָם שֶׁהֶחֱיָנוּ וְקִיְּמָנוּ וְהִגִּיעָנוּ לַזְּמַן הַזֶּה:

Boruch atto Adonoi, Elohenu melech ho'olom, she-he-ḥe-yo-nu v'ki'y'monu v'higi'onu la'zman hazeh.

Blessed art Thou, O Lord our God, King of the universe, who hast kept us in life, preserved us, and enabled us to reach this season.[1]

KIDDUSH

The special *Kiddush* for Rosh Ha-Shanah is found in the regular Prayer Book. After the *Kiddush*, it is customary

---

[1] This benediction (She-he-ḥe-yo-nu) is recited on each night of all the festivals except on the last two nights of Pesaḥ. On the second night of Rosh Ha-Shanah the recitation of this blessing takes place over new fruit.

for each one at the table to dip a bit of apple in honey and to say:

בָּרוּךְ אַתָּה יְיָ אֱלֹהֵינוּ מֶלֶךְ הָעוֹלָם בּוֹרֵא פְּרִי הָעֵץ:

יְהִי רָצוֹן מִלְּפָנֶיךָ יְיָ אֱלֹהֵינוּ וֵאלֹהֵי אֲבוֹתֵינוּ שֶׁתְּחַדֵּשׁ עָלֵינוּ שָׁנָה טוֹבָה וּמְתוּקָה:

> Blessed art Thou, O Lord our God, King of the universe, who createst the fruit of the tree.
>
> May it be Thy will, O Lord our God and God of our fathers, to renew unto us a happy and pleasant year.

GENERAL OBSERVANCE OF THE DAY

The mornings of both days are spent at the synagogue. The afternoon should be devoted to private prayers, serious reading and general reflection and conversation in harmony with the season. Among customs of the Middle Ages, still practiced by observant Jews, is that of walking beside a running stream on the afternoon of the first day of Rosh Ha-Shanah to reflect upon the purifying effect of water and to recite from Micah the verse:

> "Who is a God like unto Thee, that
> pardoneth the iniquity,
> And passeth by the transgression of
> the remnant of His heritage?
> He retaineth not His anger forever,
> Because He delighteth in mercy.

ROSH HA-SHANAH — NEW YEAR

> He will again have compassion upon us;
> He will subdue our iniquities;
> And Thou wilt cast all their sins into
>   the depths of the sea."   (7:18–20.)

This ceremony takes its name from the words of the verse, "Thou wilt cast all their sins," and is called *Tashlich* (thou wilt cast).

Chapter VIII

YOM KIPPUR — DAY OF ATONEMENT

SHABBAT SHUVAH

The Sabbath between Rosh Ha-Shanah and Yom Kippur is known as *Shabbat Shuvah*, the Sabbath of Repentance or Return, from the *Haftarah* which is read thereon, beginning with the word "Shuvah," Return.

PURPOSE OF THE FAST

The climax of the whole spiritual season is reached on Yom Kippur, the Day of Atonement. This is the holiest day of the year, the "Sabbath of Sabbaths." It is a day devoted entirely to the claims of the spirit. All bodily needs and desires are resolutely put aside, and the day becomes "The Great White Fast." It is spent in the synagogue, fasting, in confession of sin and in prayer for pardon, in acknowledgement of man's weakness and frailty, and God's majesty and glory. Yom Kippur is a striking example of the concerted effort of a whole people, regardless of time or place or

YOM KIPPUR — DAY OF ATONEMENT

personal condition, to reach up to the divine — to attain an exalted spiritual state.

The value of an annual period devoted exclusively to thoughts upon the seriousness of life and its ethical problems, to the consideration of man's proper relations towards his Creator and his fellowmen — the value of such a period is obvious, and ennoblement in some degree must follow from the proper observance of the *Yomim Noroim*, the Days of Awe.

The fast begins at sundown, which ushers in the Yom Kippur day, and lasts until the stars appear after sunset on the following day, more than twenty-four hours. It is a complete fast, not even a drop of water being permitted. This fast is commanded in the Bible as a sign of affliction (Numbers 29:7). It is, however, not to be regarded merely as a self-imposed punishment for any wrong-doing. It is rather to be regarded as the first step toward an upright life, the *mastery* of natural wants by the will, the control over impulse and desires by purpose and plan. It serves further to impress upon the mind some salutary truths. Faintness of body produces a humility of spirit, a realization of human weakness and its dependence on God's mercy for sustenance. It points to the natural equality of all men, subject to the same natural laws, and inculcates sympathy for the hungry and needy.

But the purpose of the fast is not exhausted by these lessons. The fast is intended to put the worshipper in a frame of mind susceptible to the exalted ideal of perfect righteousness that the day extols. The remarkable passages of Isaiah read in the synagogue on Yom Kippur morning contain a picture of the true kind of fast, of the true purpose of the fast.

> "Is such the fast that I have chosen?
> The day for a man to afflict his soul?
> Is it to bow down his head like a bulrush,
> And to spread sackcloth and ashes under him?
> Wilt thou call this a fast,
> And an acceptable day to the Lord?
> Is not this the fast that I have chosen:
> To loose the fetters of wickedness,
> To undo the bands of the yoke,
> And to let the oppressed go free,
> Is it not to deal thy bread to the hungry,
> And that thou bring the poor that are cast out
>   to thy house?" (Isaiah 58:5–7.)

KOL NIDRE

The Holiday is formally begun with the evening service at sunset which ushers in the tenth of Tishri. This service is called *Kol Nidre* (All Vows) from the first words of the ancient formula that begins it. Just before the *Kol Nidre*, a verse is recited by the leaders of the congregation, admitting all who desire to the prayers and services, regardless of what their relations to the Jewish community during the rest of the year might have been. The *Kol Nidre* is of great antiquity and its haunting strains awaken slumbering emotions in the Jewish heart. It

YOM KIPPUR — DAY OF ATONEMENT

pronounces a nullification of vows[1] and has for this reason been made the subject of attack by ignorant or malicious persons. However, the vows that are released by the *Kol Nidre* are only those which the individual has made to his Creator or to himself, and *not* by any means, the vows that man has made to his neighbor. Indeed the Rabbis have specifically and repeatedly stated that man must make his peace with all whom he may have wronged, intentionally or unintentionally, before he can hope to make his peace with God. However, on the basis of this formula, the trustworthiness of a Jewish oath was often assailed, so much so, that an extra oath (the Jew's oath) was required from them.

Somehow there is magic in the words *Kol Nidre* — a serious, sobering magic. It recalls the atmosphere of hushed expectancy, the feel of the crowded synagogue, visions of white-robed, swaying figures, the pleading tones of the suppliant Cantor. Daily passions and desires recede before the world of the spirit which the *Kol Nidre* conjures up.

AL ḤET

Chief among the prayers of Yom Kippur day is the confession of sin, which starts with the words *Al Ḥet* (for the sin). This confession of sin reveals the simplicity

---

[1] Vows made in the past year, in Sephardic rituals; vows to be made in the coming year in the Ashkenazic service.

THE THREE PILLARS

of Israel's dogmas, and its love and faith in God, who, besides being a righteous Judge, is thought of as a forgiving and merciful Father. As a child in grief turns naturally to its parent, so Israel, grief-stricken at its sins, turns to God whom it has offended, for mercy. No need is felt of an intermediary; no atonement is necessary other than confession of sin, reparation for the wrong and the resolve not to sin again. An erring child, returning to its yearning, forgiving father — that is the idea which underlies so many of the beautiful prayers of the day.

YIZKOR

Yizkor, or Memorial Services, are generally held during the morning services.[1] At this Service each worshipper makes mention of the name of his departed and prays for the peace of their souls. Special prayers — *El Moleh Rahamim* (God, Full of Compassion) — are also recited by the officiating rabbi, when previously requested.

NEILAH

The concluding service of the day is called *Neilah* (Closing). The service is so called from the prayer, "The Closing of the Gates," which is recited at this time.

Yom Kippur is unique in its twofold aspect of fast

---

[1] *Yizkor* Services are also held on the eighth day of Pesah, the second day of Shavuot and the eighth day of Sukkot (Shemini Azeret).

YOM KIPPUR — DAY OF ATONEMENT

and festival; for the day is indeed a festival, a time of the exultation of the spirit in the confident hope of forgiveness. Hence the color for Yom Kippur is the festal color, white, which according to the custom of the German Jews during the Middle Ages, was worn on Sabbath and holidays. The association of the shroud idea and death with the *Kittel* or white robe, is altogether out of keeping with the spirit of the day.

The services and fast are brought to an end at the appearance of the evening stars, by the recital of the first line of the *Shema*, and the triumphant declaration, "The Eternal is our God." With this assertion of the unity of God and His sovereignty over the universe, a single *Shofar* sound ushers in a new year, and life is again begun with renewed courage and idealism.

PROVISION FOR CHILDREN'S OBSERVANCE

Parents must remember that these *Yomim Noroim* are for their children also, and that they are to be given the full benefit of the spiritual values of the season. The older sons and daughters ought to have regular seats at the synagogue, so that they will not feel out of place. Each should have a good *Mahzor* with an English translation. Otherwise, they can hardly be expected to derive much moral or religious stimulation. The younger children present a problem which is solved at the synagogues in various ways, chiefly by brief services

THE THREE PILLARS

for children held at several periods during the day. Whatever the method, the children should be provided for and not be allowed to feel that the sacred day has no significance for them.

The example of older sisters and brothers will often suggest to the younger ones the idea of fasting part of the day, although it is not obligatory upon them. Children under nine years of age are forbidden to fast at all; after that time, they may begin to prepare by fasting part of the time. It is a wholesome discipline; no harm can come of it, and any attempt made along those lines before the fast becomes a duty, will make it easier subsequently. Fasting is compulsory for girls at twelve and for boys at thirteen.

GENERAL PREPARATIONS

Before lighting the candles for Yom Kippur it is customary to kindle a *Yahrzeit* light (Memorial Lamp) that is to burn through Yom Kippur day until sunset. This is done in memory of the departed, and is symbolic of immortality. *Yahrzeit* lamps in glasses, so that all danger of fire is removed, may be easily procured. Any of the candle left after Yom Kippur is used for a *Havdalah* light during the year, thus symbolically carrying into daily life, the light of the spirit and eternity.

Every thing forbidden on the Sabbath is forbidden on this great Sabbath of Sabbaths. The meal for breaking the fast should be prepared before Yom Kippur.

YOM KIPPUR — DAY OF ATONEMENT

BLESSINGS FOR LIGHTS

The lights are kindled, as for the Sabbath, with these blessings:

בָּרוּךְ אַתָּה יְיָ אֱלֹהֵינוּ מֶלֶךְ הָעוֹלָם אֲשֶׁר קִדְּשָׁנוּ
בְּמִצְוֹתָיו וְצִוָּנוּ לְהַדְלִיק נֵר שֶׁל (*on Sabbath add* שַׁבָּת
וְשֶׁל) יוֹם הַכִּפּוּרִים:

Blessed art Thou, O Lord our God, King of the universe, who hast sanctified us by Thy commandments, and commanded us to kindle the light of the (Sabbath and the) Day of Atonement.

בָּרוּךְ אַתָּה יְיָ אֱלֹהֵינוּ מֶלֶךְ הָעוֹלָם שֶׁהֶחֱיָנוּ וְקִיְּמָנוּ
וְהִגִּיעָנוּ לַזְּמַן הַזֶּה:

Blessed art Thou, O Lord our God, King of the universe, who hast kept us in life, preserved us, and enabled us to reach this season.

Grace is recited before and after the meal which inaugurates the fast. The *Kiddush* and *Zemirot* are omitted. It is customary to dip a piece of apple in honey at this meal just as on Rosh Ha-Shanah and express the hope that the year will be a happy one.

Parents bless their children before departing for the synagogue (page 71), and individuals ask each other's pardon for wrongs or unintentional offenses.

Chapter IX

PESAḤ

GENERAL SIGNIFICANCE OF PESAḤ

Passover affirms the great truth that liberty is the right of every human being. It marks the first time in the history of the world that a nation questioned the time-honored institution of slavery and actually dared to break its shackles. Israel's defiance to Pharaoh set in motion the liberty bell of humanity, proclaiming "liberty throughout the land unto all the inhabitants thereof" (Leviticus 25:10). Pharaoh has become symbolic of the oppressor and every struggle for freedom on the part of mankind is an eloquent echo of the ancient challenge to Pharaoh, "Let my people go." So synonymous are freedom and life to Israel, that the time of its freedom marks the beginning of a new life, and the month of Nisan in which Passover occurs, marks the beginning of the national year. Unlike nations who strive to hide their lowly beginnings, the Jew makes a persistent effort to remember his slavery. The redemption from Egypt, the consciousness that freedom is a divine gift, to be used for divine purposes, forms the background for many commandments and ceremonies in his daily life, and the age-old story of that redemption, becomes an ever new and all-absorbing tale. By celebrating the festival of its own freedom, the Jewish people pays homage to the great ideal of all human freedom.

VARIOUS NAMES OF THE FESTIVAL

The festival is known as *Pesaḥ*, or Passover, because the Angel of Death "passed over" the homes of the Israelites when the first-born of Egypt were slain. In the Prayer Book it is called *Ḥag Ha-Matzot*, the Feast of Unleavened Bread, with the additional phrase, "*Zeman Ḥerutenu*," the season of our freedom. Pesaḥ begins on the evening of the fourteenth day of Nisan and lasts eight days.

PREPARATIONS IN GENERAL

The preparation for the proper observance of Passover constitutes a great opportunity for the woman to contribute to the Jewish spirit of the home. Such preparations will necessarily involve extra time and effort, but the return in spiritual satisfaction and influence upon the members of the family circle will amply repay this additional expenditure of energy and time. The essential of all Passover preparations is the removal of leaven of any type from the home. Leaven has become a symbol for all that is sour and corrupt, and the home, swept bare of leaven, typifies a people cleansed from the taint of slavery and evil. Incidentally, the spirit of making things fit for Passover, of brightening up, is in harmony with the spirit of spring, and an atmosphere of freshness is procured by the thorough spring cleaning which takes place shortly before the festival.

LEAVEN OR ḤOMETZ

By leaven or *Ḥometz* is meant any substance that sets up or is intended to set up a fermentation or produces any chemical change in the way of souring. *Ḥometz* includes all kinds of cereals such as wheat, barley, oats, rye and spelt which ferment, and baking-powder, yeast, baking-soda, and starches. Foods made of leaven or containing even the slightest particle of leaven are forbidden on Passover. In addition, many other kinds of food, apparently free of any leaven are prohibited, due to the apprehension that such foods may have come in contact with leaven in the process of picking, drying or packing. Foods such as prunes and raisins[1] that have been picked, dried and packed under special supervision for Passover purposes, as well as milk, butter

---

[1] Fresh string-beans, peas and even rice are used on Pesaḥ by the Sephardic (Spanish and Portuguese) Jews, but not by the Ashkenazic Jews.

and canned goods thus especially supervised may be used.[1]

KASHERING

There should be separate sets of household utensils and dishes for Passover. However, there are certain utensils used during the rest of the year which may be made fit for Passover use, by special *kashering* for the occasion. The idea underlying all *kashering* is absolute cleanliness and the removal of all leaven or contact with leaven. *Kashering* may be effected either by glowing or purging (sterilization). To procure a glow, the object is heated to a red heat till it emits sparks. To sterilize, the object is placed and allowed to remain for a minute in boiling water. The water should overflow or bubble over. This overflow is hastened by depositing in the boiling water some glowing coals or a small piece of red-hot iron. After the purging, it is customary to rinse in cold water.

Bearing in mind the purpose of the process, which is to remove all traces of leaven or contact with leaven, it becomes apparent that dishes of earthenware or other absorbent material, or utensils of any substance so dented or cracked or glued, that any part of them is inaccessible

---

[1] One should be careful to purchase *Matzoh*, wine, and other Passover supplies from reliable sources. Those shopkeepers who are willing to make a financial sacrifice to keep the Sabbath and observe Jewish law are entitled to this patronage.

to the flame or the water, do not come within the class of objects which can be made fit for Passover use by *kashering*. Objects that cannot be thoroughly cleansed before purging, such as a grater, sieve, bread-basket or narrow-necked bottles, may not be submitted to the process. Perfectly whole vessels, of one piece and of metal, may be *kashered*, but not those of wood, earthenware or agate. Dishes which come in direct contact with the fire, as frying-pans, require glowing.

IMMERSION OF GLASSWARE

Glassware should be immersed and covered with fresh cold water for three days, the water being changed each day shortly before nightfall. Silver that is flat and of one piece, may be rendered fit by purging. One should not purge any object unless twenty-four hours have elapsed since leaven was used therewith.

BEDIKAT ḤOMETZ, SEARCH FOR LEAVEN

In order to be sure that no *Ḥometz* of any kind has been overlooked in places where it was used during the year, it is customary to make a thorough search in the home on the evening before Pesaḥ, just after dark. This ancient tour of investigation is performed by candle-light. Before making the search, it is customary to place bits of bread in those places where bread has been frequently seen during the year, so that the searchers may find them. A wooden spoon and feather used by the searchers to collect the bits of bread add to the quaintness of this ceremony. These should all be gathered up, and burned the following morning before ten o'clock. After the search, the following formula is pronounced:

כָּל חֲמִירָא וַחֲמִיעָא דְאִכָּא בִרְשׁוּתִי דְּלָא חֲמִתֵּהּ
וּדְלָא בְעַרְתֵּהּ לִבָּטֵל וְלֶהֱוֵי כְּעַפְרָא דְאַרְעָא:

All manner of leaven, that is in my possession, which I have not seen nor removed, shall be null and accounted dust of the earth.

The children will enjoy participating in the search, hiding the bread and lighting the way. This ceremony is usually conducted by the father of the home; in his absence, by the mother.

MO'OS ḤITTIM

A good old Jewish custom and one very much in keeping with our modern ideas of social service, is *Mo'os Ḥittim*, the provision of *Matzoh* and other holiday necessities for those who are still in the bondage of poverty. A contribution to a fund for this purpose or a personal gift to the needy is a very logical part of Passover preparations.

THE THREE PILLARS

GENERAL HOLIDAY PREPARATIONS

For Pesaḥ, like the other festivals, preparation should be made in the way of marketing, candle lights (page 86) and *Eruv Tavshilin* (page 85) when necessary.

FESTIVAL LIGHTS

The lights should be kindled on the first two nights and the last two nights of the festival with the appropriate benedictions (page 86).

On the first two nights of Passover it is customary to add the last blessing on page 87.

The second evening marks the beginning of the counting of the Omer (page 111).

Kiddush is recited by the master of the home. It will be found in the *Haggadah*.

THE SEDER

The *Seder* service, held on the first and second nights of Passover, is one of the most appealing of our many beautiful ceremonies. Its voice goes out to turn the heart of the wanderer homeward, and its call reaches even the indifferent. There are few who can resist its charm and under the influence of its simple ceremonies, we re-live our own childhood. The past of our people lives again and we live in it. The Hebrew word *Seder* means

HAGGADAH

The special service book used is the *Haggadah* (the Recital), so called because it relates the story of the redemption, with appropriate prayer and praise.

The barest *Seder* table is beautiful on Passover, for beauty is inherent in the *Seder* service. But to the spiritual charm of the *Seder*, artistic beauty must be added also, and for this we look to the mother, who prepares the home and the table for the ceremony.

The *Seder* commemorates the night of the departure from slavery to freedom, and the symbols that were prominent that memorable night in Egypt, the *Pesaḥ*, the *Matzoh*, and the *Moror*, are still prominent on our tables today. Indeed, it is around these three symbols that the whole *Seder* service is built. The meaning of these three symbols is as follows:

PESAḤ, PASCHAL LAMB

The *Pesaḥ*, or roasted lamb-bone, together with a roasted egg — The lamb-bone is in memory of the *Pesaḥ* or paschal lamb sacrificed and partaken of, by the Israelites, on the eve of their departure from Egypt. The lamb was sacred to the Egyptians, and its blood, sprinkled on the door-posts of the Israelites, declared defiance to the gods of their oppressors and to all Egyptian traditions. The paschal lamb was offered regularly at this season during the time of the Temple in memory of this event. The roasted egg recalls the sacrifice that was offered in the Temple by the individual worshipper on every festival — the festival offering or the *Ḥaggigah* — and it voices the prayer for the restoration of the glory of Israel, its national life and institutions. This feeling finds expression also in the spontaneous exclamation at the end of the *Seder*.

לְשָׁנָה הַבָּאָה בִּירוּשָׁלָיִם

L'shonoh ha-bo-oh bi-rusholoyim

"Next Year in Jerusalem."

MATZOH, UNLEAVENED BREAD

The *Matzoh,* or Unleavened Bread — The Bible carefully explains that this is the bread of affliction, the bread of poverty and haste, made by our ancestors for the paschal sacrifice before the departure from Egypt. It is even now used by the toiling poor of eastern countries who have time only to prepare and snatch a hurried meal.

PESAḤ

MOROR, BITTER HERBS

Moror — The Bitter Herbs which, together with the *Pesaḥ* and *Matzoh*, formed the paschal meal eaten in Egypt before the Exodus, were symbolic of the bitterness of the bondage that was to end that night.

ADDITIONAL SYMBOLS

To these three basic symbols, tradition has added others. The *Ḥaroset*, a thick mixture of grated apples, powdered cinnamon, chopped nuts and wine, is taken to represent the bricks that the Israelites made. The salt water is poetically described as typifying the salty tears shed by the mothers upon hearing Pharaoh's cruel command that the male infants were to be drowned. The parsley or other green vegetable dipped into the salt water probably represents the beginning of the ancient meal and corresponds to the modern *hors d'oeuvres*.

The four cups of wine that are used correspond to the four different expressions for freedom mentioned in the story of the Exodus.

THE OPEN DOOR

The Cup of Elijah is the extra cup of wine for a needy stranger or unexpected guest. There is a tradition that the visitor may even be Elijah, the prophet. This mysterious champion of Israel appears in time of distress

THE THREE PILLARS

to fight the cause of his people. He may enter the Jewish home in the guise of a stranger, leaving his blessing. Hence at one point in the *Seder*, the door is opened to admit the homeless and also the prophet Elijah, who may be waiting among them.[1]

The coming of the prophet is also closely connected with the coming of the Messiah and the final redemption of all mankind from misery and sin.

CHILDREN AND THE SEDER

The *Seder* service should be made an occasion of joyous family reunion, of spiritual beauty, and an opportunity for the renewed expression of Jewish emotions. The service as conducted by the head of the house is for the entire household. The children occupy an exalted position at the *Seder*. Indeed, the Talmud states that the *Seder* service was planned especially to impress and inspire them. To be sure, many of the incidents, such as the *Mah Nishtanoh* (the four questions), the four sons, the four cups, the hiding of the *Afikomen*, the rhymes,

---

[1] Our bitter history has given this simple ceremony of opening the door an additional significance. The door is opened so that all who wish may come and see just how the *Seder* is conducted, and realize how horribly false and groundless has been the accusation that Jews use Christian blood at the *Seder* services. However unthinkable it may appear that anyone could accuse the Jews of such a thing, the number that were tortured and put to death for this wild charge, which might be launched by any benighted peasant and find ready credence, is appalling.

and the refrains, tend to support such an opinion as does the very character of the service itself, which is in the form of *Haggadah*, or story telling.

Each *Haggadah* has the simple directions that are necessary for the conducting of a *Seder* and outlines the ceremonies step by step. It is a wise parent who awards a handsome gift for the recital of the *Mah Nishtanoh*, for the return of the *Afikomen*, for the fine reading of selected passages and for intelligent questions. He realizes that the *Seder* may be made such an epoch in the child's life, that its happy memory becomes an inspiration to conduct *Sedorim* of his own when the time comes.

SYNAGOGUE SERVICES

Services are held on the evenings of the festival, before sundown, at the various synagogues. These are usually attended by the fathers and sons while mothers and daughters are busy preparing for the *Seder*. There are regular holiday morning services at the synagogue, the first two and last two days of Passover, at which the attendance of the entire family is desirable. It will add to the interest and benefit of the attendance to equip each member with a Passover Prayer Book (*Mahzor*) where the special service may be followed. These books are comparatively inexpensive and make desirable holiday gifts.

HOL HA-MOED

The intermediate days of the festivals of Passover and of Sukkot (that is, the time between the first two days and the last two days) are called *Ḥol Ha-Moed*, or secular days of the festival, and are considered as semi-holidays. While ordinary daily occupations are performed, the sanctity of the festival is maintained to some extent and the mother will have to exercise her ingenuity to add those little touches to the service, menu and general routine to help the family remember that it is still *Yom Tov*.

Chapter X

SHAVUOT

OMER

There are forty-nine days between the second day of Passover and Shavuot. On the second day of Passover, an Omer or measure of the grain from the new spring harvest was brought to the Temple as an offering. From the day on which the Omer was brought, the Israelites had to count seven weeks, or forty-nine days, the fiftieth day being Shavuot (the Feast of Weeks), or Pentecost (the fiftieth, in Greek). Although the bringing of the Omer ceased with the destruction of the Temple, these forty-nine days between Passover and Shavuot are still counted. These days are therefore called the *Sefirah* days (counted days) or *Omer* days.

This period has proved an unhappy one in Jewish life. The Hadrianic persecutions in the second century occurred in their worst form at this season. To add to the almost unbearable misery, a devastating plague broke out among the rabbis and scholars, thinning their ranks considerably. In later years too, the horrors of the Crusaders reached their climax during these days. So they have always remained tinged with sadness.

Hence the prohibition of marriage and public or even private celebrations. However, there are several days when these restrictive measures do not apply; namely, the thirty-third day of the Omer (Lag ba-Omer), when the plague during Hadrian's time abated; on Rosh Ḥodesh Iyar and from Rosh Ḥodesh Sivan until Shavuot.

FESTIVAL OF FIRST FRUITS

The beautiful festival of Shavuot with its associations of golden fields, of peaceful reapers and its echoes of thundering Sinai is observed on the sixth and seventh day of Sivan. It is first, the festival of the wheat harvest and the season of the offering of the first fruits in the Temple. In Palestine the grain harvest lasted seven weeks. It began with the harvesting of the barley shortly before Passover and ended with the commencement of the wheat harvest at Pentecost, the wheat being the last cereal to ripen. At this time too, the people began to make their pilgrimages to the Temple (Deuteronomy 26:1–11) and there offered the first fruits of the harvest. Hence the holiday is also called the Season of the First Fruits.

ANNIVERSARY OF THE REVELATION

But Shavuot, like Pesaḥ, is an historic as well as an agricultural festival. It is the anniversary of the giving of the Law at Mount Sinai; hence it is called in the

SHAVUOT

Prayer Book "the Season of the Giving of our Law." Passover has been poetically described as the day of the betrothal of Israel and God. Carrying out the figure, Shavuot may be called the wedding day, the time when Israel was wedded to God, by His revelation on Mount Sinai. It marks the birthday of Israel's spiritual freedom. This event, of such tremendous consequence to all mankind, is commemorated annually. The celebration of the festival stimulates renewed allegiance to the Torah of Israel, to those laws which have become the foundation for the morality of civilized humanity and which hold in their essence the spirit of that ideal world toward which civilized man is constantly striving.

BOOK OF RUTH

There are services at the synagogue evening and morning. The Book of Ruth is read during one of the morning services,[1] not only for the breath of nature it carries, but because Ruth, the Moabitess, accepted the Torah given to Israel at this season. There are some who read in this custom, a tribute to the power of the Jewish woman to preserve the Law. The Messiah will be a descendant of David, who was a scion of Ruth, and the custom seems to say that every woman, while she may not give to the world the Messiah, can still do much

---

[1] The Sephardim read the book at the afternoon services, one-half each day.

toward the preservation of the people from whose midst he will come.

Many synagogues have introduced Confirmation Services, or Consecration Services for children entering Hebrew School, either on Shavuot itself or a day close to it. Since Shavuot is the anniversary of the giving of the Law, it is deemed an appropriate time for the younger generation formally to express their allegiance to it. In harmony with the spirit of spring, and the agricultural origin of the festival, it has long been customary to decorate the synagogue with foliage and flowers. The women of the congregation usually undertake this pleasant duty, and the daughters too, ought to be allowed to do their part toward beautifying the house of worship.

GENERAL PREPARATIONS

Milk foods seem to be popular during Shavuot. This custom probably had its origin in the practice of serving coffee, cake and other milk dishes, late in the evening, to those who remained awake to study the Torah, on the first night of Shavuot.

For Shavuot, like the other festivals, preparation should be made in the way of marketing, candle lights (page 86), and *Eruv Tavshilin* (page 85) when necessary. It is customary to have flowers and growing plants in the home. These are also appropriate for gifts as holiday greetings.

Chapter XI

SUKKOT

SIGNIFICANCE OF THE FESTIVAL

Sukkot is the festival commemorating the last of the three pilgrimages to the Temple, which the people made annually to bring a voluntary offering of thanksgiving, for the blessings that had been bestowed upon them. These pilgrimages occurred at the end of the successive harvests; the barley harvest at Passover; the spring wheat at Shavuot, and the fall harvest of produce and fruits at Sukkot. All these seasons were times of gladness, but Sukkot marked the rejoicing at its height. It represented the natural joy of an agricultural people, that sees its granaries full and its harvests successful. The season is characterized in the Prayer Book, by the term *Zeman Simḥotenu*, the time of our gladness, and the festival is also called "The Feast of the Ingathering."

Another aspect of the festival is portrayed by its name, *Ḥag Ha-Sukkot*, the Feast of Booths. For *Sukkah* means booth and Sukkot is the Feast of Booths or Tabernacles, commemorating God's watchful care over

THE THREE PILLARS

the Israelites as they dwelt in frail booths in their journey through the wilderness.

DIVISIONS OF FESTIVAL

Sukkot comes on the fifteenth day of Tishri and lasts seven days. The seventh day is *Hoshanah Rabbah* (the Day of the Great Hoshanahs). The eighth day is a separate festival called *Shemini Azeret*, the Eighth Day of Solemn Assembly, and the ninth is known as *Simḥat Torah*, the Day of Rejoicing of the Law. *Simḥat Torah* is also an occasion in some synagogues for Consecration Services for children entering Hebrew School.

The nature of the festival is both agricultural and historic, and its ceremonies are also of an agricultural and historic character. The *Lulav* represents the produce of the earth and the *Sukkah* commemorates the dwelling in booths.

THE LULAV AND ETROG

The *Lulav* (literally palm branch) has bound with it, branches of myrtle and willow. The fourth plant is a species of the citron family, the *Etrog*. These four typical plants of the land of Palestine are taken to represent the entire realm of natural produce, and are symbolic of God's universal sovereignty and man's dependence upon Him.

SUKKOT

Tradition is very rich in further explanations of the meaning of the *Lulav*. These plants are said to typify the human body: the upright palm, the spine; the citron, the heart; the small oval-shaped myrtle leaf, the eye; and the longer oval, the willow leaf, the mouth. And the human body, like the plants that typify it, fulfills its highest function in the service of God. Another interpretation is that these plants typify various classes found in human society.[1] There are those who, like the citron, have both fragrance and sustenance value — that is, learning and good deeds; those who, like the myrtle, have fragrance but no sustenance value — learning but no good deeds; those who, like the palm (date palm), have no fragrance but sustenance value — no learning but deeds of goodness; and finally, those who, like the willow, have apparently neither sustenance value nor fragrance — neither learning nor piety. Yet all of these plants are necessary and when bound together, the one makes up the deficiencies of the other. Even as in all the other realms of God's creation, so in human life, each has his use and purpose. "Each thing is needed by each one; nothing is good or whole alone" — that is the message of the *Lulav*.

---

[1] Israel Abrahams: *Festival Studies*, p. 123 and ff.

THE THREE PILLARS

BLESSINGS FOR THE LULAV AND ETROG

The following benediction should be pronounced every day of Sukkot (except the Sabbath) at home or in the synagogue, while holding the *Lulav* and *Etrog*.

בָּרוּךְ אַתָּה יְיָ אֱלֹהֵינוּ מֶלֶךְ הָעוֹלָם אֲשֶׁר קִדְּשָׁנוּ
בְּמִצְוֹתָיו וְצִוָּנוּ עַל נְטִילַת לוּלָב:

Blessed art Thou, O Lord our God, King of the universe, who hast sanctified us by Thy commandments, and hast commanded us concerning the taking of the Lulav.

On the first day of the festival (unless it is the Sabbath) add:

בָּרוּךְ אַתָּה יְיָ אֱלֹהֵינוּ מֶלֶךְ הָעוֹלָם שֶׁהֶחֱיָנוּ וְקִיְּמָנוּ
וְהִגִּיעָנוּ לַזְּמַן הַזֶּה:

Blessed art Thou, O Lord our God, King of the universe, who hast kept us in life, preserved us, and enabled us to reach this season.

If the first day is Sabbath, add above on second day.

THE SUKKAH

Sukkot is the season when the Jew is required to dwell in booths. How much could be written on the symbolism of the Sukkah! Frail as all earthly power, open to the

SUKKOT

sky as a constant reminder of God's watchful protection, a mixture of sunshine and shadow as life itself; like Israel, at the mercy of every ill wind, yet appearing year after year, speaking of the final restoration of "the fallen Sukkah of David," indestructible in spirit like the Jewish people, and as rich in significance. The hope of this final restoration has never left the Jewish heart. It was this hope that sustained the homeless Jew as he built his tiny Sukkah in the Ghetto, rejoiced without a harvest and dreamed of the time when he might again observe Sukkot in the land of his fathers.

Yet the Sukkah today is simply another illustration of how the beautiful and expressive symbols of Jewish life must lie mute and ignored, unless the Jewish woman will breathe into them the breath of life and love.

The ideal arrangement is a Sukkah for every home, and the minimum is the community or synagogue Sukkah, where all may enjoy Sukkah hospitality. Decorating a Sukkah is one of those occasions when duty is so pleasant that it becomes a privilege. Once the rough frame has been erected, it is for the women and children to cover it with foliage, decorate it with fruits and flowers, making it as artistically beautiful as possible. And it should be a matter of pride and friendly rivalry to make "our Sukkah" the most beautiful. Open house, or rather open Sukkah, is the rule during the festival and Sukkah hospitality to friends and strangers, rich and poor, has become proverbial. In these days of

THE THREE PILLARS

porches, patios and car-ports, it is not hard to find a place to erect a Sukkah. A little enthusiasm will overcome any local difficulties.

Where the climate permits, people live in the Sukkah for seven days according to Biblical law. However, everyone ought at least to visit a Sukkah, partake of some refreshment and pronounce the proper benedictions.

On entering the Sukkah the following is recited:

בָּרוּךְ אַתָּה יְיָ אֱלֹהֵינוּ מֶלֶךְ הָעוֹלָם אֲשֶׁר קִדְּשָׁנוּ בְּמִצְוֹתָיו וְצִוָּנוּ לֵישֵׁב בַּסֻּכָּה:

Blessed art Thou, O Lord our God, King of the universe, who hast sanctified us by Thy commandments, and commanded us to dwell in the Tabernacle.

If the entrance is for the first time, add:

בָּרוּךְ אַתָּה יְיָ אֱלֹהֵינוּ מֶלֶךְ הָעוֹלָם שֶׁהֶחֱיָנוּ וְקִיְּמָנוּ וְהִגִּיעָנוּ לַזְּמַן הַזֶּה:

Blessed art Thou, O Lord our God, King of the universe, who hast kept us in life, preserved us, and enabled us to reach this season.

ḤOL HA-MOED

The period between the first two and the last two days is called *Ḥol Ha-Moed*. The last day of *Ḥol Ha-Moed*, or the seventh day of Sukkot is known as *Hoshanah*

SUKKOT

Rabbah, the day of the Great Hoshanah, for on this day, the *Hoshanahs* (prayers beginning with "*Hoshanah*," "Save us") are recited. A very interesting ceremony, dating back to prophetic times, took place at the morning service. In the Temple, on this day, a great and very solemn procession of people carrying large branches, slowly walked around the altar, the boughs swaying as in a gentle rain. Undoubtedly there is some connection here with rainfall because the prayers for rain (*Geshem*) are recited on Shemini Azeret, the following day. To this day, little willow branches, also called "Hoshanahs" are held and shaken during the reading of the Hoshanahs in the synagogues.

SHEMINI AZERET

The eighth day is a separate festival, the day of Solemn Assembly and is observed, like all other festivals for two days.

SIMḤAT TORAH

The second day of Shemini Azeret is called Simḥat Torah (Rejoicing of the Law) because on that day the synagogue reading of the Torah, the five books of Moses, is completed and the reading begun again. This notable event is celebrated by seven joyful processions (*Hakkafot*) in the synagogue, led by the men bearing the *Sefer Torah*s.[1] The children take part in these processions, following the Scrolls of the Law, carrying flags and joining in the songs of praise and rejoicing.

To enter into the real spirit of Simḥat Torah, one must understand the place of the Torah in the Jewish heart. For the term *Torah* means more than a code of laws, albeit divine in origin and hence perfect. It means more than the study and instruction necessary to its understanding and application in life. It means more than disinterested devotion to truth, to knowledge for its own sake, an ideal toward which the expression *Torah Lishmah* (Torah, truth for its own sake), so frequently used in Jewish life, testifies. It means more than the gathered wisdom of its many interpreters. For the *Torah* as conceived by the Jew, contains in its essence all wisdom, divine as well as human. It is the embodiment of the sum total of eternal truth and knowledge. "Turn it over and over again," say the Sages, "for everything is in it" — everything.

The utmost that the wisest of mortals can do, is to express and develop in accordance with the innate character of the Torah, some infinitesimal part of the wisdom therein contained — to isolate, as it were, one drop in the vast ocean of divine omniscience, to analyze

---

[1] These seven processions are patterned after the processions around the city of Jericho. See Joshua 6.

SUKKOT

that and from its constituent elements approach an understanding of the whole. What wonder then that the Jew, full of awe and reverence, devoted a special day to rejoicing over his Torah, to the expression of his overflowing love. And so the festive season always dignified and restrained, closes on the high key of renewed allegiance to the God of righteousness, whose laws sustain the spirit of man as well as his body.

GENERAL PREPARATIONS

For Sukkot, like the other festivals, preparation should be made in the way of marketing, candlelight (page 86) and *Eruv Tavshilin* (page 85) when necessary.

Chapter XII

ḤANUKKAH

ISSUES OF THE ḤANUKKAH STRUGGLE

The festival of Ḥanukkah is perhaps one of the most popular in the Jewish calendar; popular with the young, for it grips the emotions and fires the imagination; popular with the mature, for its idealism and far-reaching consequences. For this festival commemorates one of the most unequal struggles and brilliant victories in the history of the world; a victory fraught with momentous import to the future development of civilization. The events of this absorbing story of sublime faith and valor are related in great detail in the first and second Books of Maccabees in the Apocrypha. The significance of these events, however, can only be appreciated in the light of subsequent history. For in this warfare between Jew and Greek, there were arrayed against each other not only their respective armies, but their respective cultures and civilizations. It was a conflict between the polytheism of Greece and the monotheism of Judea, between the ethical concepts of the Greek and the ethical concepts of the Jew.

ḤANUKKAH

Judaism possessed some ethical concepts which were distinctly Hebraic in character and altogether out of keeping with the spirit of Hellenism. For instance, such ideas as the paramount importance of duty, of sacrifice, of negation and inhibition, of renunciation and spiritual discipline were altogether foreign to the Greek point of view.

Civilization today would have been totally different had Judea been defeated. We do not know to what end a degenerated Hellenism would have led us, but it is from the spirit of Hebraism, from its ideals, that those forces are derived which influence men's lives today. Christianity, Mohammedanism, and Judaism, the three great religions of civilized mankind are the products of these Hebraic concepts, triumphant on the battlefield of Judea against the Greek aggressors.

Moreover, the issues of that conflict are issues that are still paramount today, and precious to the heart of every civilized man. Chief of these issues was the principle of religious freedom. While this principle is universally admitted today, it has taken mankind more than two thousand years to establish it as the inalienable right of every human being. It was the small commonwealth of Judea that first formulated this principle and fought for its establishment.

When the observance of the Sabbath, the dietary laws and the Abrahamic Covenant were forbidden by the tyrant Antiochus it was the principle of religious freedom which was defied, and it was for the establishment of this freedom that the Maccabees fought. Not only the Jewish people, but all peoples are indebted to the Maccabees for having so valiantly championed this great cause.[1] The Festival of Lights, therefore, commemorates not a Jewish victory alone, but a victory for mankind. The right to worship one's own God in one's own way is the keystone of the great arch of civilization, and the essential condition for human progress.

The second great issue for which the Maccabees fought was the right of cultural self-determination. Every people has the right, and even more, the duty, to preserve its own customs and culture. Civilization is a composite of the various heritages of the literature, art and wisdom of many nations, whose great men spoke in diverse tongues but in universal accents. The world cannot afford to lose the contribution of any of its geniuses, whatever their nationality. The Jews at the time of the Maccabees, while possessing great admiration for Greek civilization, still maintained that the destruction of their own culture or that of any other people, was not necessary to the preservation of Greek culture. Other cultures had a right under the sun and were of equal, if not greater, service to mankind.

And finally there was involved in the conflict between the Greek and the Jew, the right to moral

---

[1] In its early history, the Church celebrated the feast of the Maccabees.

ḤANUKKAH

self-determination. Every people has evolved its own standards of ethics and morality. These standards find expression in its laws, customs, traditions, and institutions. The absolute right, no nation has yet embodied in concrete practice. Mankind has thus far attained only an approximation of the absolute right. This approximation is the result of the sum total of the combined ethical visions of the seers of all nations. The chief contribution to the moral vision of mankind was made by the prophets of Israel. And were it not for the Maccabees, this contribution would have been destroyed. The passion for right and social justice was predominantly the product of the Jewish genius and not of Greek civilization.

The festival of Ḥanukkah, or Dedication, is celebrated on Kislev the twenty-fifth and lasts for eight days, the time it took Judas Maccabeus and his heroic followers to rededicate the Temple after it had been cleansed from heathen pollution. Tradition relates also that the single cruse of holy oil unearthed, containing oil sufficient for only one day, miraculously lasted for eight days.

THE MESSAGE OF THE ḤANUKKAH LIGHTS

Ḥanukkah is frequently called the Festival of Lights from the practice of kindling lights, one on the first evening and one more for each succeeding day until the eighth. As these lights are kindled and grow brighter day by day, they become for the Jewish people, little flames of faith, faith that liberty in all its aspects, religious, cultural, and intellectual, will one day become the unchallenged right of every human being. They represent faith in the ultimate triumph of all righteous causes in spite of whatever odds may be arrayed against them. They symbolize the steady march of truth, the growth of the light of Israel's law of love and justice, the ultimate victory of all forces of light over darkness.

The characteristic ceremony of Hanukkah is the kindling of these Hanukkah lights. No Jewish home should be "in darkness" on the Festival of Lights.

Where the Hanukkah lights burn, there the light of Judaism still lives. They proclaim that the season of rededication means for the Jew two things. It means his own rededication to the religious and ethical ideals of his fathers, and the rededication of the people as a whole, to the reclamation of the land of their fathers in which these ideals found their first and fullest expression.

BLESSINGS FOR THE HANUKKAH LIGHTS

In many homes each child has a separate Menorah to light and all are kindled together. In others, the children take turns in lighting the one Hanukkah lamp. Whatever the arrangements may be, they should be made to feel that their presence and participation are of the utmost

HANUKKAH

importance. Following are the blessings for lighting the Ḥanukkah lights as soon as the evening stars appear.

בָּרוּךְ אַתָּה יְיָ אֱלֹהֵינוּ מֶלֶךְ הָעוֹלָם אֲשֶׁר קִדְּשָׁנוּ בְּמִצְוֹתָיו וְצִוָּנוּ לְהַדְלִיק נֵר שֶׁל חֲנֻכָּה:

Blessed art Thou, O Lord our God, King of the universe, who hast sanctified us by Thy commandments, and commanded us to kindle the light of Ḥanukkah.

בָּרוּךְ אַתָּה יְיָ אֱלֹהֵינוּ מֶלֶךְ הָעוֹלָם שֶׁעָשָׂה נִסִּים לַאֲבוֹתֵינוּ בַּיָּמִים הָהֵם בַּזְּמַן הַזֶּה:

Blessed art Thou, O Lord our God, King of the universe, who hast wrought miracles for our fathers in days of old, at this season.

On the first night add:

בָּרוּךְ אַתָּה יְיָ אֱלֹהֵינוּ מֶלֶךְ הָעוֹלָם שֶׁהֶחֱיָנוּ וְקִיְּמָנוּ וְהִגִּיעָנוּ לַזְּמַן הַזֶּה:

Blessed art Thou, O Lord our God, King of the universe, who hast kept us in life, preserved us, and enabled us to reach this season.

MO'OZ TZUR

The Ḥanukkah song, *Mo'oz Tzur* (Fortress, Rock of My Salvation), can be secured in convenient form with

English, Hebrew, transliteration and music. The children will like to play the melody on their musical instruments.

HANUKKAH AND CHRISTMAS

Hanukkah frequently occurs very close to Christmas. Christmas is a Christian festival, properly celebrated by Christians, but not by Jews. Christmas trees, gifts or parties have no place in a Jewish home. Jewish children ought not to participate in school plays or other celebrations of this season. Parents should take the opportunity afforded by the Hanukkah festival to make the children glory in their own traditions and happy that they are Jews. Hanukkah affords an ample opportunity for the exchange of gifts, Hanukkah parties, and other expressions of love and goodwill. Children who attend the religious schools of the community will in all likelihood have Hanukkah plays and treats provided for them. Indeed, this is one of the seasons of the year when the actual value of attending religious schools stands out most convincingly to the juvenile mind. Where there are no organized religious schools, any mother with a little initiative can secure a cast for a Hanukkah play, from among the children's friends, and organize a Hanukkah entertainment for the small community which would otherwise be without one. Appropriate reading for the day is the Hanukkah story found in the two

ḤANUKKAH

books of the Maccabees, in the Apocrypha, or in Josephus.

When it is borne in mind that the most faithful Jew is the one who knows enough of his people's history to glory in it, that the most observant Jew is the one who finds real joy in its ceremonies, then only does the full opportunity for renewed Jewish loyalty that lies in the festival of Ḥanukkah and its proper celebration become apparent.

CHAPTER XIII

PURIM

ORIGIN OF PURIM

The Jewish woman seems to have appropriated Purim for herself. A woman is the heroine of the occasion; the dramatic settings and situations are entirely after the feminine heart; the method of celebration, of "sending portions to one another and gifts to the poor," is essentially womanly. She has entered heartily into the traditional spirit of the day which requires her to exercise all skill in the culinary arts, in the preparation for a party (*Se'udah*) and general merry-making. She is expected to attend Purim services, where the events which led to the institution of Purim are publicly read.

Purim, which is celebrated annually on the fourteenth day of Adar, commemorates the events related so graphically in the Book of Esther, the *Megillah* or Scroll containing the story. The word Purim means *lots*, and the day is so called, after the lots cast by Haman, for a favorable time to carry out his evil intentions. But the celebration of Purim means more than the commemoration of this particular escape from destruction through

PURIM

an unexpected deliverance. Israel's experience with Haman repeated itself frequently in Jewish history. As the Passover *Haggadah* has it, "For not only one enemy, but in every generation have there arisen those who would destroy us, but the Holy One, Blessed be He, hath delivered us from their hands." It is interesting to note that besides the Purim that is universally celebrated on the fourteenth day of Adar, there are many local Purims, days devoted to the celebration of the deliverance of some particular community from some impending disaster.[1]

READING THE MEGILLAH

The day before Purim is known as *Ta'anit Esther* (Queen Esther's Fast) for reasons given in the story. The fast ends and Purim begins at nightfall, with the reading of the *Megillah* in the synagogue. It is a specific obligation to hear the *Megillah* (Book of Esther) read in the

---

[1] For instance, in Florence, Italy, there is a special Purim, celebrated on the 27th of Sivan because on that day in 1790, the Jews of Florence were singularly saved from the hands of a mob. On Purim day itself in 1840 at Rhodes, the Jews were vindicated of a charge of murder for which many of them had been imprisoned and tortured. Hence Purim in that city is celebrated as a double festival. In 1595, the accidental discharge of a cannon by a Jewish woman brought victory to the Turks against the Spaniards and rescue to the Jews in a fortress on the island of Chios. The day is still celebrated by the Jews of Chios and is called the Purim of Chios.

original tongue. Anyone unable to follow the Hebrew recital should read the story in the language which she can understand.

The method of celebrating Purim is characteristic. It finds its expression on this occasion, as on many others, in terms of social service, a method as old as the Jew himself. For the Jew never lived for himself alone. At the synagogue, the half shekel is collected for the poor; and gifts (*Shalaḥ Monos*) are exchanged among friends. To add to the general sum of happiness by remembering some of the local institutions, the federated charities, and institutions in Israel, is the real Purim spirit.

MODERN STROLLING PLAYERS

The custom still exists in many places of masking and dressing up. Companies of youthful Purim players, "less interested, it must be admitted, in art than in the pecuniary rewards that are likely to follow their efforts," go from house to house, causing merriment and bustle, coaxingly announcing, "Today is Purim, tomorrow it's out; give us some pennies and put us to rout!" The occasion produces, too, a large crop of Purim plays, sometimes surprisingly well performed by ambitious actors in the Hebrew schools. Gold crowns, purple robes and long black beards are in great demand, together with supplies of candy for the audience, the children of the schools. Purim furnishes an opportunity to satisfy the

PURIM

child's heart, to make him really glad that he is a Jew. Many of the holydays carry with them prohibitions; there are so many "don'ts" that involve sacrifices on his part. But here is an opportunity for joy unalloyed. There are no "don'ts" in Purim. It is one of the occasions when heart's desires may be granted. Purim and Ḥanukkah can be made red-letter days in childhood's calendar. A little of the time and ingenuity that go into the making of Halloween costumes and Valentine parties may well be applied to Purim costumes and Purim parties. Such efforts will result in increased Jewish interest on the part of the children and prove a means of stimulating their Jewish spirit.

THE SE'UDAH

The evening meal at the end of the first day of Purim is known as the *Se'udah*. It is a religious feast generously interspersed with merriment. The ability to find everything in daily secular life holy, and nothing in the religious life out of harmony with human necessities and desires, is well shown by the spirit that pervades the *Se'udah*. It is a religious ceremony, but it is a party, a party at which a sanctimonious air and solemn sentiments are altogether out of place. The proper spirit is, the more merriment, the more merit!

THE THREE PILLARS

SHUSHAN PURIM

The fifteenth day of Adar is known as Shushan Purim from the fact that the holiday was celebrated a second day in Shushan, the scene of the Purim story, as related in the *Megillah*.

Of course, Purim means a goodly supply of *Hamantaschen*, Haman's pockets or Haman's ears, so called from the triangular shape of these cakes, filled with poppy seeds, jellies and other delicious concoctions. Tradition backs up these cakes for Purim just as in American life, it calls for turkey and cranberry sauce for Thanksgiving. Any Jewish cook book contains approved recipes for making *Hamentaschen*.

PURIM GREETINGS

"Merry Purim," "Happy Purim" are the greetings exchanged on this occasion, and it is a merry Purim only when it has been made a happy Purim for the family and for others.

Chapter xiv

TISHA B'AV

EVENTS COMMEMORATED

Tisha b'Av, the ninth day of Av, is a most unhappy day in Jewish experience. On it, both the first and second Temples were destroyed, the first in 586 B. C. E. by the Babylonians under Nebuchadnezzar, and the second in 70 C. E. by the Romans under Titus. The destruction of the Temples meant to the Jewish people the destruction of their religious center and the end of their political autonomy. This national catastrophe has never been forgotten, even as the hope of a return has never left the Jewish heart. According to tradition, the Messiah, who will in due time restore all of Israel to its homeland will be born on the very day which twice marked the fall of Israel. The consolation of the Messianic hope has helped to sustain the spirits of a broken people, who annually commemorate the Great Black Fast. The Rabbis say that all the signs of mourning which are observed at a personal bereavement ought to be observed on this day, with double intensity. They hold that every Jew should place the welfare and interests of his people above his own and feel that a national calamity is to each individual member of the Jewish people a far more grievous sorrow than any personal bereavement might be.

Thus, on Tisha b'Av, Jews the world over, those in free countries and those who are still oppressed, join with their brethren in fasting and in mourning. The day is spent in reading the *Kinot* (special dirges lamenting the destruction of the Temple); and depicting the sufferings of those who witnessed the desolation of the land, grieving with Jeremiah over the fallen walls of Jerusalem (Lamentations), fasting and praying that God may restore His people. Tisha b'Av is really a Jewish Memorial Day. It is a day devoted to the memory of the departed glory of ancient Israel, to a contemplation of its long and bitter martyrdom, to the whole miracle of its survival.

THE NINE DAYS

The period from the first to the ninth of Av is known as the "Nine Days." These days are characterized by a subdued atmosphere. Weddings and other public functions of a joyous character are prohibited. Strict Jewish observance forbids the enjoyment of meat or wine or the donning of new clothing.

THE THREE WEEKS

There are many who begin this annual period of mourning, not on the first day of Av, but on the day the first breach was made in the walls of Jerusalem, the seventeenth of Tammuz, just three weeks before the ninth of Av. Hence this period from the seventeenth of Tammuz to the ninth of Av, is known as "The Three Weeks." Observance during this period is of the same general character as during the last nine days, differing, however, in some minor details. Marriage is forbidden during "The Three Weeks."

THE JEWISH WOMAN AS A CONSTRUCTIVE FORCE

The proper observance of Tisha b'Av may well result in an increased enthusiasm for the Jewish renaissance in Israel. This rebirth of Jewish life and culture in Israel ought to appeal strongly to the Jewish woman. Throughout the Tisha b'Av literature, Zion is compared to a woman, stripped of her glory and deserted. It is the *daughter* of Zion who is forsaken and the *mother* Zion who mourns for her children. Is it too much to suggest that the daughters and mothers today busy themselves with the healing of the "daughter of my people," and do their share in bringing to a nearer realization the words of the prophets:

> "Comfort ye, comfort ye, my people,
> Saith your God,
> Bid Jerusalem take heart,
> And proclaim unto her,
> That her time of service is accomplished...."[1]
>
> (Isaiah 40:1-2)

---

[1] These words begin the prophetic section read on the Sabbath following Tisha b'Av. This Sabbath is called *Shabbas Naḥamu*, the Sabbath of Consolation, after the opening words, "Naḥamu," "Comfort ye."

Chapter XV

SEMI-HOLIDAYS AND MINOR FASTS

ROSH ḤODESH

There are several occasions during the year which call for special mention, besides the holidays already enumerated. Among these is *Rosh Ḥodesh*, the day of the new moon. This day was regarded originally as a solemn occasion. It marked the beginning of a new period and as such was "calculated to arouse serious thoughts in the minds of the Israelites." It marked the rapid flight of time, yet it offered a fresh chance for a new and better life. Thus solemn as the new moon was, it bore an aspect of gladness and of fresh hopefulness. Both the serious and hopeful nature of the occasion are reflected in the service in the synagogue. On the Sabbath before the new moon, a special prayer is recited in which the name of the coming month and the days upon which it occurs are announced. The prayer embodies the hope that the new month may be a time of blessing and good for all Israel, a period characterized by reverence for the Divine and the dread of sin. Tradition has made

SEMI-HOLIDAYS AND MINOR FASTS

Rosh Ḥodesh, the day or days on which the new moon falls, a semi-holiday for the women.

LUNAR AND SOLAR CALENDARS

Perhaps a word ought to be said in reference to the lack of correspondence between the Jewish and non-Jewish calendar. Everyone is familiar with the fact that Rosh Ha-Shanah, which always falls on the first day of Tishri in the Hebrew calendar, may fall in September one year and perhaps in October, the following. Like Rosh Ha-Shanah all the other Jewish holidays occur at fixed dates in the Hebrew months, but their secular equivalents may vary from year to year. This will be understood, if it is borne in mind that the Jewish calendar is lunar, that is, based on the phases of the moon in combination with seasonal changes, while the secular calendar is solar, based on the relation of the sun to the earth. The Jewish year is composed of lunar (moon) months. The time it takes the moon to pass through its various phases, serves as the measure of a month. This time is twenty-nine days, twelve hours and a fraction of an hour. The month is either twenty-nine or thirty days long, depending upon the exact moment that the new moon appears. Twelve moon or lunar months or three hundred and fifty-four days make up the Jewish year.

The secular year is solar, based on the phases of

the earth's rotation about the sun. It takes three hundred and sixty-five days to complete the cycle of these phases. Hence the secular year is three hundred and sixty-five days. This makes the Jewish year a little more than ten days shorter than the secular year. It is this discrepancy of about ten days a year between the two calendars, that makes the Jewish holidays "movable" as far as the secular calendar is concerned.[1]

In order to equalize the years, a leap month[2] of thirty days is added to the Jewish year every second or third year to make up for this deficiency of thirty days, lost at the rate of ten days a year. The year having a leap month is a leap year. In a lunar cycle of nineteen years, the following are leap years, having an extra month added, the third, sixth, eighth, eleventh, fourteenth, seventeenth, and nineteenth.

A knowledge of the names of the new months and the days when they occur, will help to adjust the mind to the orderly routine of the Jewish year and to the sequence of the various festivals. It will also help to understand the calendar of the Jewish year, the *Luaḥ*, and facilitate the finding of the equivalent secular date

---

[1] It is interesting to note that the Church still has some festivals regulated by the lunar system, which are called "movable feasts" due to the fact that their dates are not fixed but vary in the calendar of the solar system.

[2] The leap month (Second Adar) is added after the twelfth month Adar, approximately February-March.

SEMI-HOLIDAYS AND MINOR FASTS

of a birth, Bar Mitzvah or Yahrzeit. Jewish calendars are as easily obtained as English ones, and there are some very fine ones with both Jewish and secular dates and all Jewish and secular holidays tabulated. Obviously, no Jewish home should be without one of these aids to Jewish life and observance.

TU B'-SHEVAT

Tu b'-Shevat (sometimes referred to as *Ḥamisho 'Osor b'-Shevat*), that is, the fifteenth day of the month of Shevat, corresponds to Arbor Day. It marks the time when the sap begins to run again in the trees in Israel and the day is known as the New Year of the Trees. It is celebrated by devoting special attention to nature, by the planting of new trees and by the enjoyment of the various kinds of fruit that grow in Israel.

With the renewal of interest in Israel, through the courageous effort on the part of world Jewry in re-establishing the national homeland, this festival of the Jewish Arbor Day has assumed a larger significance and has become symbolic of the planting and growth of new life in the land. It is a beautiful custom on the part of Jews the world over, to send contributions to Israel at this season through the Jewish National Fund, for the purchase of land and the planting of trees, in their own name or in memory of some loved one. Sometimes this is done too, at the birth of a child, at marriage or upon any occasion to be commemorated in a poetical, and yet practical way.

Mothers should see that the day does not pass unnoticed, by arranging parties and serving special fruits for the occasion, such as nuts, dates, figs, *Bokser* or carob, and raisins, especially the Israeli products.

MINOR FASTS

Aside from the fast days in the Jewish year which have already been mentioned[1] there are a few occasions, each commemorating an historic event of dire significance for the Jewish people, that ought to be remembered in the Jewish home. Surely an abstinence from festivity, the absence of special luxuries in food or dress, and a thought or two devoted to the occasion are the least observance required on days of such character. The proper method of observing these days is a fast beginning at sunrise and lasting until the appearance of the evening stars.

Among these days is the tenth day of Tevet commemorating the beginning of the siege of Jerusalem which led eventually to the fall of the first Temple. Another is the seventeenth day of Tammuz to commemorate the first breach made in the walls of Jerusalem by Nebuchadnezzar. With this day begin the three

---

[1] Yom Kippur, Tisha b'Av and Queen Esther's Fast.

SEMI-HOLIDAYS AND MINOR FASTS

weeks of mourning for the destruction of Jerusalem which end on Tisha b'Av, the ninth day of Av.

The third day of Tishri commemorates the murder of Gedaliah, scion of a noble and pious family, appointed governor of Judea by Nebuchadnezzar after he had conquered the land. Under his protection, peasants, laborers, and military men returned and resettled the land. When he was slain through treachery, those who had returned to the land became terrified and departed, thus making complete the dispersion of the Jews.

Chapter XVI

DEATH

JEWISH ATTITUDE TOWARD DEATH

The Jew tries to look at death steadily and fearlessly. He does not attempt to pass over its agony or try to minimize its bitterness and pain. Grief is so natural that it must be respected. No effort should be made to stem the springs of human emotion. "Do not attempt to comfort thy friend, while his dead is before him," is the admonition of the Rabbis in the *Ethics of the Fathers*. However, after the first rush of grief, any attempt at comfort and consolation becomes not only a humane service but a religious duty.

CONSOLATION OF IMMORTALITY

Judaism seeks a ray of light and reassurance in the darkness of death and finds it in the belief in God's beneficent purpose, in His loving direction of all human existence and in the underlying conviction of a future life. These feelings are expressed in the words spoken

DEATH

when one learns of a death, "Blessed be the righteous Judge" and "The Lord hath given and the Lord hath taken; blessed be the name of the Lord."

JEWISH BURIAL

The first concern of the immediate mourners is the proper interment of the body, and until this duty has been performed, they are exempt from certain religious obligations such as attending services, prayer or study. The body is prepared for burial according to prescribed Jewish law (*Taharah*) and is buried as soon after death as possible, in a shroud of white linen. However, burial may be delayed for a day or two, to await mourners, to conclude preparations, or for any cause that may add to the honor of the dead. The Jew buries his dead in accordance with the verse recited during the burial service, "And the dust returneth to the earth as it was and the spirit returneth unto God Who gave it." (Ecclesiastes 12:7.) Cremation is not a Jewish practice.

CUSTOMS IN THE HOUSE OF MOURNING

After death, a light is kindled at the head of the bier to symbolize the light of the soul or its immortality. A light is also kept burning in the home throughout the *Shiva* week.

THE KERIAH

The *Keriah* is a deliberate tear made in the outer garment of the immediate mourners and all who were present at the time of death. Rending the garment is an oriental method of expressing grief. It is striking to note that the *Keriah* or tear in the garment, must be made by the mourner standing up, not seated or lying down as if to impress the fact that the storms and sorrows of life must be met bravely, standing up, and that one is not to lie down in utter despair under them. More recently, it has become acceptable to wear small strips of cloth in which a tear is made, as a substitute for the actual tear in the garment.

Mourning is obligatory for the death of a parent, child, sister, brother, husband or wife. It is true, of course, that one cannot rejoice or mourn simply because it is obligatory. These must necessarily be spontaneous emotions. However, it is natural to assume that death would cause the deepest sorrow to those most closely related to the deceased. Hence these close relatives are required to mourn.

SHIVA WEEK

After the burial, the *Shiva*, the seven day period of deep mourning begins. During the *Shiva* week, it is customary to sit on low chairs, avoiding the more luxurious cushions or armchairs. The first meal eaten upon the return from the cemetery is the *Shiva* meal, or meal of condolence,

DEATH

usually prepared by friends. The meal includes eggs, the ancient symbol of immortality. It is very much in order for friends to help with the preparation of food in the house of mourning, or to bring in foods which they have cooked. It is not good taste, or appropriate, however, to bring elaborate or expensive boxes of candy, fruit, and similar delicacies.

Mourners are not expected to leave the house of mourning during the *Shiva* week, except for the Sabbath services. Hence, services are held at the home of mourners morning and evening, to give them an opportunity to worship with a *Minyan* and to recite the *Kaddish*. The *Shiva* week is devoted to mourning, to quiet meditation and study that the heart may be eased of the burden of its emotion and the mind adjust itself to take up life under the new conditions. This is the time when human sympathy and comfort are real acts of mercy, affording temporary relief by directing the thoughts to other channels. The utmost care and tact are required not to force oneself upon the mourner, to wait for his speech and to withdraw immediately should it become evident that he would rather be alone.

When entering the house of mourning, sorrowing friends are often at a loss how to express their sympathy. This need is filled by the words of consolation with which it is the custom to greet the mourners: "May the Lord comfort you, together with all the mourners of Zion and Jerusalem."

THE THREE PILLARS

THE KADDISH

The *Kaddish* (or Sanctification) is a prayer glorifying God and expressing submission to His will. It is a prayer for the establishment of His kingdom "in your lives and in your days, and in the life of all Israel." It contains no mention of death. It is an exalted expression of faith and adoration, that rises above personal sorrow and bereavement. This prayer is recited at the end of each of the three daily services, every day for eleven months by the sons of the dead. Where there is no son, it is said by the daughters, or anyone who wishes to pay a loving tribute by its recitation. The *Kaddish* is not said at home in private prayer. It must be recited with a *Minyan*, that is, with ten men constituting a congregation.

WEARING BLACK APPAREL

There is no law commanding the mourner to wear black. Indeed some pious people object to it, saying that death is the entrance into a new and better life, and does not call for gloominess or a gloomy color. However, it is the custom in western countries, and the personal feeling of the individual ought to decide the question.

SHELOSHIM

The second period of mourning begins at the close of the *Shiva* week and ends one month, or thirty days,

DEATH

after the death. This period is known as the *Sheloshim*, meaning thirty. During the *Sheloshim*, the general conduct of ordinary affairs is resumed. However, actions permitted during the rest of the first year, such as a marriage when conditions make it pressing, are prohibited during the *Sheloshim*. The mourning period continues until the close of a full year.

THE TOMBSTONE

The time for the setting of the tombstone depends upon local custom. In some countries it is set as soon after the burial as possible, in others, at the end of the eleventh month or shortly before the year has elapsed.

THE YAHRZEIT

The anniversary of the death is known as the *Yahrzeit*. The occasion is commemorated by the recital of the *Kaddish* at the evening and morning services, and the giving of charity. A memorial lamp is kept burning from sunset to sunset. By some the day is observed by fasting and special prayer.

All the observances of burial and mourning, such as the burning of the memorial lights, the *Keriah*, the *Kaddish*, the wearing of black, and the tombstone are to be regarded simply as customs designed to express and relieve the surcharged emotions. These things should not be allowed to become objects and rites of superstitious awe, especially with children among whom there may be such a tendency. "You do not feel more tenderly for him than I do," our Rabbis represent God as saying to the living, about the dead. While there may be great sorrow, there cannot be room for terror or despair.

It is becoming more and more the custom to pay tribute to the dead by the establishment of memorials. These memorials often take the form of memorial rooms, beds in hospitals and kindred institutions, synagogue windows, memorial libraries, the endowment of a chair in an institution of Jewish learning, or the purchase of land and the planting of groves of trees in Israel.

MENTIONING THE DEAD

In speaking of the dead, it is customary to add, during the first year especially,

עָלָיו הַשָׁלוֹם

Olov Ha-Sholom

May his soul rest in peace

or

זֵכֶר צַדִיק לִבְרָכָה

Zecher Tzadik Li-V'rochoh

The memory of the righteous is a blessing

Chapter XVII

ISRAEL REBORN

Nineteen hundred years lie between the year 70 of the Common Era when the Roman legions put an end to the Second Jewish Commonwealth and 1948 when the Third Jewish Commonwealth was born.

The new commonwealth, the State of Israel, is engaged in a heroic struggle to solve many complex human, economic and political problems. It stands as a symbol and a reality in our modern age, exciting our wonder and interest, turning our attention back to the earliest days of Jewish history when our people was first born.

It was on the soil of Israel that its deep spiritual, religious, and national character reached its fullest maturity. It was in the land of Israel that the Jewish people achieved independence and created a distinctive culture. Here the great patriarchs, prophets and poets enunciated ideas of universal and eternal appeal. Here the Bible was written. Exiled from Palestine, the Jewish people never ceased to remain faithful to the goal of return, and never ceased to pray for the restoration.

From their earliest periods of separation, the sojourn in Egypt, the captivity in Babylon, through endless wanderings in many lands among conflicting cultures, Jews recited parable and piyut, responded to the yearnings of their fellow Jews, and recalled the promise to Abraham:

"And I will give to thee and to thy seed after thee the land of thy abode — all the Land of Canaan for an everlasting possession and I will be their God." — (Genesis 17: 8.)

Their strong attachment to the Holy Land, their zealous insistence upon Hebrew prayers; their building a "fence around the Torah," helped spur their commitment to the "Return to Zion." With the onset of modern political Zionism, Jews in many parts of the world became alerted to the necessity of reestablishing a Jewish national home in the ancient homeland, "to create for the Jewish people a home" in Palestine secured by international law.[1]

After the period of *Aliyot*, the Mandatory government, World War I and World War II, many "papers" and "commissions," and after the catastrophic holocaust of 6,000,000 of European Jewry, after intensive fighting in Palestine, the new State of Israel proclaimed its independence on May 14, 1948.

Jews all over the world are mindful of the remarkable opportunities for spiritual growth and human development which this new state offers. American Jewish

---

[1] Zionist Congress adopted this aim in 1897.

women particularly recognize the unique obligation which rests upon them. Through their various social service, Zionist, religious and philanthropic organizations, they have pledged support to Israel.

Loyal and devoted as the American Jewish woman is to her American heritage, responsible citizen in her native land, vigilant in her regard for democratic survival, active politically on local, national and international levels — she is nonetheless greatly concerned with the survival and progress of the State of Israel.

Through her dedication to traditional practices in her home, her passionate concern for her children's Hebrew education, her high regard for the synagogue, the Jewish woman will more fully understand the spiritual import of the State of Israel, and will see herself as a link in the 4000 year old chain that began with the Hebrew matriarchs.

S. B. L.

CALENDAR — *LUAH*

5718 (1957–58) to 5723 (1962–1963)

	5718 **1957**	5719 **1958**	5720 **1959**	5721 **1960**	5722 **1961**	5723 **1962**
Rosh Hashanah (First Day)	Sept. 26	Sept. 15	Oct. 3	Sept. 22	Sept. 11	Sept. 29
Yom Kippur	Oct. 5	Sept. 24	Oct. 12	Oct. 1	Sept. 20	Oct. 8
Sukkot (First Day)	Oct. 10	Sept. 29	Oct. 17	Oct. 6	Sept. 25	Oct. 13
Shemini Azeret	Oct. 17	Oct. 6	Oct. 24	Oct. 13	Oct. 2	Oct. 20
Simhat Torah	Oct. 18	Oct. 7	Oct. 25	Oct. 14	Oct. 3	Oct. 21
Hanukkah (First Day)	Dec. 18	Dec. 7	Dec. 26	Dec. 14	Dec. 3	Dec. 22
	1958	**1959**	**1960**	**1961**	**1962**	**1963**
Purim	Mar. 6	Mar. 24	Mar. 13	Mar. 2	Mar. 20	Mar. 10
Pesah (First Day)	Apr. 5	Apr. 23	Apr. 12	Apr. 1	Apr. 19	Apr. 9
Shavuot (First Day)	May 25	June 12	June 1	May 21	June 8	May 29

All Jewish Holy Days and religious festivals, as well as the weekly Sabbath, begin on the preceding evening at sunset.

CALENDAR — *LUAḤ*

5724 (1963–64) to 5729 (1968–1969)

	5724	5725	5726	5727	5728	5729
	1963	**1964**	**1965**	**1966**	**1967**	**1968**
Rosh Hashanah (First Day)	Sept. 19	Sept. 7	Sept. 27	Sept. 15	Oct. 5	Sept. 23
Yom Kippur	Sept. 28	Sept. 16	Oct. 6	Sept. 24	Oct. 14	Oct. 2
Sukkot (First Day)	Oct. 3	Sept. 21	Oct. 11	Sept. 29	Oct. 19	Oct. 7
Shemini Azeret	Oct. 10	Sept. 28	Oct. 18	Oct. 6	Oct. 26	Oct. 14
Simḥat Torah	Oct. 11	Sept. 29	Oct. 19	Oct. 7	Oct. 27	Oct. 15
Hanukkah (First Day)	Dec. 11	Nov. 30	Dec. 19	Dec. 8	Dec. 27	Dec. 16
	1964	**1965**	**1966**	**1967**	**1968**	**1969**
Purim	Feb. 27	Mar. 18	Mar. 6	Mar. 26	Mar. 14	Mar. 4
Pesaḥ (First Day)	Mar. 28	Apr. 17	Apr. 5	Apr. 25	Apr. 13	Apr. 3
Shavuot (First Day)	May 17	June 6	May 25	June 14	June 2	May 23

All Jewish Holy Days and religious festivals, as well as the weekly Sabbath, begin on the preceding evening at sunset.

INDEX

Arba Kanfot 26

Bar Mitzvah 33
Bat Mitzvah 36
Bentschen Gomel 24
Berachot 20
Bible 59
Brit Milah 30
Burial 147

Calendar
    explanation 141
    ten-year 156
Confirmation 36, 114
Consecration 114

Day of Atonement 90
Death 146
Dietary laws 40

El Moleh Raḥamim 94
Eruv Tavshilin 85

Grace 25

Haggadah 105, 109
Ḥallah 27, 69
Ḥamisho 'Osor b'-Shevat 143
Ḥanukkah 124

Havdalah 75
Ḥometz 100

Israel 153

Kabbalat Shabbat 74
Kaddish 150
Kashrut 42
Keriah 148
Kiddush 72
Kol Nidre 92
Kosher, meaning of 42

Leaven 100
Luaḥ 156

Maḥzor 57
Marital Laws 38
Marriage 37
Megillah 132
Memorial services 94
Mezuzah 19
Minor fasts 144
Minyan 34
Motzi 20
Mourning 147
    apparel 150

Name, choice of 31
    naming girls 32

INDEX

New Year 82

Omer 111

Parvah 47
Passover 98
Pesaḥ 98
Pidyon Ha-Ben 33
Prayer
    private 51
    services 50
Purim 132
Rosh Ha-Shanah 77
Rosh Ḥodesh 140

Sabbath 67
    preparation for 69
    eve services 70, 74
    morning services 74
    candle lighting 70
Seder 104
Sefirah 111
Seliḥot 79
Services
    morning 56
    afternoon 56
    evening 57

Se'udah 135
Shabbat Shuvah 90
Shavuot 111
She-he-ḥe-yo-nu 87
Sheloshim 150
Shemini Azeret 121
Shiva 148
Siddur 55
Simḥat Torah 121
Sukkah 118
Sukkot 115
Symbols
    American 15
    Jewish 17
    religious 17

Tashlich 89
Tefillin 35
Terefah 43
Tisha b'-Av 137
Tombstone 151
Tu b'-Shevat 143

Yahrzeit 151
Yizkor 94
Yom Kippur 90
Yomim Noroim 78, 95